Dorothy M. Miner

Airedale Terriers

Everything about Purchase, Care, Nutrition, Breeding, Behavior, and Training

With full-color photographs

Illustrations by Pam Posey-Tanzey

BARRON'S

Photo Credits

Duff M. Munson: pages 8, 12 bottom, 24, 45 top, 52, 53, 56, 65 top, 68, 72, 81, 85; Paola Visintini: pages 9, 12 top, 20, 41, 84; Jean Wentworth: pages 13 top, 28; Toni Tucker: pages 13 bottom; Dee Ross: pages 16, 29, 57, 60, 61 top, 64, 65 bottom; Bob Schwartz: pages 25, 45 bottom, 61 bottom; Chris Halvorson: pages 33, 73, 89. Photos on page 93 courtesy of William Secord Gallery.

Cover Photos

Front cover: Toni Tucker; Back cover: Dee Ross; Inside front cover: Duff M. Munson; Inside back cover: Paola Visintini.

All inquiries should be addressed to:
Barron's Educational Series, Inc.
250 Wireless Boulevard
Hauppauge, NY 11788

http://www.barronseduc.com

International Standard Book No. 0-7641-0307-5

Library of Congress Catalog Card No. 98-10543

Library of Congress Cataloging-in-Publication Data
Miner, Dorothy M.
   Airedale terriers : everything about purchase, care, nutrition, breeding, behavior, and training / Dorothy M. Miner ; with full-color photographs ; illustrations by Pam Posey-Tanzey.
       p.   cm.—(A complete pet owner's manual)
   Includes bibliographical references and index.
   ISBN 0-7641-0307-5
   1. Airedale terrier. I. Title. II. Series.
SF429.A6M54   1998
636.755—dc21   98-10543
                                          CIP

Printed in Hong Kong

987654321

The Author

Dorothy M. Miner has been involved in one aspect or another of the dog fancy for over 25 years, mostly with Airedale Terriers. She has earned Obedience titles on several breeds, including Airedale Terriers, Border Terriers, a Brussels Griffon, Bulldog, and Pembroke Welsh Corgi. She also trains and competes in AKC Tracking events with her dogs, and her Airedale, Jeep (U-CD Elliot's Tuffenuff Jeep, CDX TDX), was the first Airedale to earn the title Tracking Dog Excellent. Her Airedale Possum (Kudos Country Possum, CDX) has appeared on stage with the Palo Alto Childrens' Theater as Sandy in both *Annie* and *Annie Warbucks*. She finished a breed championship on one Border Terrier and two of her Borders earned their Certificates of Gameness in American Working Terrier Association den trials. Dorothy Miner has taught all levels of Obedience training for over 20 years. To date, over 200 Airedales and their owners have participated in her classes. She is an American Kennel Club Tracking Judge (Emeritus), and a member of the Airedale Terrier Club of America's Hunting and Working Committee.

In her "other life," Dorothy Miner is a Code Enforcement Officer for the City of Palo Alto, California.

Important Note

This pet owner's guide tells the reader how to buy and care for an Airedale Terrier. The author and the publisher consider it important to point out that the advice given in the book is meant primarily for normally developed puppies from a good breeder—that is, dogs of excellent physical health and good temperament.

Anyone who adopts a fully grown Airedale should be aware that the animal has already formed its basic impressions of human beings. The new owner should watch the animal carefully, including its behavior toward humans, and, if possible, should meet the previous owner. If the dog comes from a shelter, it may be possible to get some information on the dog's background and traits there. There are dogs that, as a result of bad experiences with humans, behave in an unnatural manner or may even bite. Only experienced owners who have re-homed such dogs should consider adopting them.

Caution is further advised in socializing a dog with other dogs or with children and in exercising the dog without a leash.

Even well-behaved and carefully supervised dogs sometimes do damage to someone else's property or cause accidents. It is therefore in the owner's interest to be adequately insured against such eventualities, and we strongly urge every dog owner to purchase a liability policy that covers the dog.

Contents

There is a revival at this time to restore the Airedale's status as a sporting and hunting dog.

Preface

Take equal parts of intelligence, strength, heart, and loyalty. Add a generous portion of humor, sensitivity, and high energy. Throw in a pinch of stubbornness and feistiness. Pack this inside a handsome 50- to 70-pound (23–32 kg) dog, and you have the Airedale Terrier.

The Airedale Terrier is a rugged, energetic fellow. Its wiry coat is reddish tan or brown with a distinctive black or dark grizzle saddle, and its bushy beard, eyebrows, and leg furnishings give it the jaunty look of an English country squire. In the show ring the Airedale presents a "top hat and tails" type of image, but in reality it is more of a "blue jeans and T-shirt" type of character. Its intelligence is considerable; its courage is legendary.

On the noble end of the scale, Airedales are fearless protectors of home and family, the ablest of hunters, and the handsomest of show dogs. On the other end, they have been willing assistants to British game poachers, participants in rat-catching competitions, and fuzzy-haired scourges of neighborhood cats. In the middle you have a beast with a sometimes perverse sense of humor that takes to heart its job of seeing that its owner doesn't take himself or herself too seriously. If Airedales were human, they would be physicists, revolutionaries, or cartoonists. They are bright, clever, independent, and not just a little manipulative. They may not be the perfect breed for everybody, but for many there is no equal. Once you've owned an Airedale you'll either never want another one, or no other breed will do.

Acknowledgments

I would like to thank my friends in the California Airedale Terrier Club who generously shared their expertise, information, and tales with me, especially Karen and Jeff Lapierre (Kudos Airedales), Samantha Curran (Evermay Airedales), Georgia McRae (Brisline Airedales), and Duff Munson, photographer extraordinaire. Thanks also to my mother and my sister, Margaret and Lori Miner, for reading and rereading the seemingly endless drafts, and my friend Beth Greenwell for moral support and perfect whiskey sours. Thanks also to the 200-plus Airedales and their owners who have gone through my obedience training classes for teaching me to think like an Airedale. Finally, thank you to my present crew of rather peculiar and much-loved four-footers: Jeep, Possum, and Pip, for keeping me entertained!

Dorothy Miner

The Airedale Terrier: Ruggedness, intelligence, loyalty, personality, and energy.

Introducing the Airedale Terrier

The Airedale Terrier is not an ancient breed; it was developed only slightly over a century ago. Originally developed as a hunting terrier, the Airedale retains the tenacity and independence that were so desirable in a dog expected to be able to tackle any type of foe, from its original quarry of rats, badgers, foxes, and otters to its more recent use on mountain lions, wild boar, and bear. Most Airedales lead a much tamer existence now, but those traits that were so valuable in a sporting terrier serve to endear it to those who have chosen it as a pet and companion. Airedales have been the pets of presidents, paupers, and Olympic stars. They have belonged to such luminaries as President Warren Harding, actor John Wayne, and author John Steinbeck. There is a resurgence in their popularity as hunting and working dogs, and they are seen increasingly more frequently as obedience and agility trial competitors. Today, Airedales serving as Pet-Assisted Therapy dogs comfort hospitalized children, the elderly in nursing homes, and youngsters in juvenile halls. They work as Search and Rescue dogs that handle rugged wilderness searches as capably as dangerous rubble searches in the aftermath of earthquakes and bombings. From stylish show dogs to fuzzy house pets, there are Airedales serving any function we can ask of our breed. President Theodore Roosevelt is quoted as saying: "An Airedale can do anything any other dog can do and then whip the other dog if he has to." Add a loyal and loving devotion toward the people they love and you have a good description of today's Airedale Terriers.

If you choose to share your life with an Airedale, don't expect a dog that will lie quietly by the fireside all day. An Airedale expects to be a part of its owner's life, and expects its folks to be active. Life with an Airedale is anything but boring!

The History of the Airedale Terrier

The Airedale Terrier has its roots firmly embedded in English soil. Its birthplace is the valley of the Aire River in Yorkshire, an industrialized area that also provided ample opportunities for the sport of hunting small game in the neighboring moors, woods, and lowlands. Even the large rats populating the factory and mill districts provided formidable opponents for the terriers of the day. Well-to-do hunters of the era were typically accompanied by a pack of hounds and several terriers, often running them

Early sporting terrier going to ground.

both together. The hounds would scent and pursue the quarry and the terriers would "go to ground" or enter into the quarry's burrow and make the kill. Terriers were often the sporting dog of choice for the common man. Early sporting terriers needed to be big enough to tackle the quarry, but not so big as to prevent them from maneuvering through the quarry's underground lair. Obviously these terriers had to have a very high degree of courage and pluck to face the foe in a tight, dark underground den without the help of human handlers.

Developing the Terrier

During the middle of the nineteenth century regular sporting events took place along the Aire River in which terriers pursued the large river rats that inhabited the area. A terrier was judged on its ability to locate a "live" hole in the riverbank and then, after the rat was driven from its hole by a ferret brought along for that purpose, the terrier would pursue the rat through water until it could make a kill. As these events became more popular, demand arose for a terrier that could excel in this activity. One such terrier was developed through judicious crossings of the Black-and-Tan Terrier and Bull-and-Terrier dog popular at the time with the Otter Hound. The result was a long-legged fellow that would soon develop into the dog we recognize today as the Airedale Terrier. This character was too big to "go to ground" in the manner of the smaller working terriers; however, it was good at everything else expected of a sporting terrier, and it was particularly adept at water work. This big terrier had other talents in addition to its skill as a ratter. Because of an infusion of hound blood it was blessed with the ability to scent game and the size to be able to tackle larger animals. It became more of a multipurpose terrier that could pursue

game by powerful scenting ability, be broken to gun, and taught to retrieve. Its size and temperament made it an able guardian of farm and home. One of the more colorful, but less-than-legal, uses of the early Airedale Terrier was to assist its master in poaching game on the large estates that were off-limits to commoners. Rabbits, hare, and fowl were plentiful, and the Airedale could be taught to retrieve game killed by its master, or to pursue, kill, and bring it back itself.

Early Names

The large terriers that originated in the region of the Aire River valley were first called "Waterside Terriers" or "Bingley Terriers." As they became more popular the name "Airedale Terrier" was settled upon, since this was more reflective of their general area of origin. There were most likely breeds other than the old broken-haired Black-and-Tan Terrier, Bull Terrier, and Otter Hound thrown into the mix in the development of the Airedale, but exactly who and what will probably never be known. Some say that the Irish and Welsh Terriers played a part in the making of the Airedale. Others say that the old Southern Hound, Welsh Hound, and Bloodhound may have been involved. There were even hints that Collie and Sheepdog blood may also have been added. Whatever the combinations were, the result was a broken-coated, long-legged game terrier that most likely weighed in at about 40 pounds (18 kg). Today, a 40-pound Airedale Terrier would appear quite diminutive, but in the mid-nineteenth century it was a very large terrier indeed.

The Early Days of the Airedale in America

The first Airedale known to arrive in the United States was a dog named Bruce, brought from England by C. H. Mason of Bradford, Yorkshire. Bruce

Many breeds went into the creation of the Airedale Terrier.

was a large, ambitious enterprise and many of the trainers were Native Americans, the most famous being the Olympic star Jim Thorpe. There was even a professional football team owned by Mr. Lingo named, naturally, the "Oorang Airedales." Jim Thorpe was a member of this team, and he occasionally referred to himself as "just an Airedale." Many handlers of hunting Airedales wanted a much larger dog than seen in the show ring. Oorang Airedales, for example, ran from small 35-pound (16 kg) dogs up to huge 100-pounders (45 kg). A split began to develop early on between the "sporting Airedale" and the "show Airedale" factions in the United States, with one difference being the size of the dog. One of the problems seen with the overly large sporting Airedales was a distinct loss of type. These dogs often appeared more houndish in appearance than their standard-sized cousins. There is a revival in the breed at this time to restore the Airedale's status as a sporting and hunting dog. Dogs from several of today's good show lines are proving themselves able workers in the field, and we are again seeing 50- to 70-pound (23–32 kg) dogs that excel in both the show ring and the sporting field.

War Dogs

Many breeds of dogs, including Airedales, were recruited for use by the United States military as war dogs. In the early days of World War II, Airedales were actively recruited, along with Boxers, Standard Poodles, Border Collies, various retrievers, and the more popular German Shepherd Dogs and Doberman Pinschers, but by the end of that war, Airedales were not used frequently in wartime employment. They were occasionally used as police and guard dogs in the United States, although they have been overshadowed by German Shepherd

made an appearance in the show ring, winning a class for Rough-Haired Terriers in 1881. The breed quickly took firm hold here. The Airedale Terrier Club of America, the parent club of the breed in this country, was established in 1888.

While the Airedale Terrier was becoming firmly entrenched in the United States as a show dog, other Americans rapidly discovered the hunting prowess that had been bred into the dog. The early history of the Airedale in America would not be complete without mentioning the significance this played in the breed's popularity. Several lines of hunting Airedales developed in the United States, with one of the most famous historically being the "Oorang" Airedale strain founded by Walter Lingo in Ohio. The Oorang Kennels

Dogs, Doberman Pinschers, and Rottweilers.

The popularity of the American Airedale Terrier peaked in the 1920s when it became one of the most popular purebred dogs in the country. Sadly, such fame also brings a downside. Less-than-scrupulous breeders in the mid-twenties produced litter after litter, with little thought to the dogs' health and temperament. Many older folks remember the Airedales of those times as tough, aggressive, often unpredictable dogs that developed a reputation for being biters and fighters. Only a truly dedicated core of Airedale breeders lovingly brought the breed back into the wonderful dog it is today.

The Airedale in Other Countries

The Airedale's popularity spread in other countries as rapidly as it did in England and the United States. Its career as a show dog was well established in England by the late nineteenth century, and it was a popular farm dog, sporting dog, and pet. Several European countries, notably England, Russia, and Germany, also recognized this dog's abilities as a superb working animal and recruited it into military service during World Wars I and II. Airedale war dogs served as sentries, messengers, guards, patrol dogs, munitions carriers, search dogs, ambulance dogs, and camp rodent exterminators.

One of the foremost proponents of the breed as a working war dog and police dog was Colonel Edwin Hautenville Richardson, one of Britain's most talented dog trainers during the early part of this century. The Airedale's considerable talents and its size, strength, intelligence, and courage made it Richardson's personal favorite working breed.

Airedales were also widely used as police dogs throughout Europe, Great

Airedales are popular throughout Europe.

Britain, and Japan. The Germans initially considered Airedale Terriers one of the top three police dog breeds, along with German Shepherd Dogs and Doberman Pinschers. Airedales are still seen as frequent competitors in working trials in these countries as well as in conformation shows. German Airedales are commonly seen in conformation shows and in Schutzhund (obedience, tracking, and protection) trials today, with many German dogs having both conformation and working titles.

The popularity of the Airedale Terrier is well established throughout Europe, Great Britain, Australia, Japan, Canada, Mexico, South Africa, South America, and, of course, the United States. It is assured of continued popularity.

Considerations Before You Buy

Is This the Right Breed for Me?

Airedale aficionados will be the first to tell you this breed isn't for everybody. Airedales are remarkably strong for a medium-sized breed, strong-willed, and above all, they are terriers. Terriers are known for their high activity level, feistiness, noisiness, and independence. Airedales need considerable amounts of exercise, regular grooming, firm but kind training, and patience. They are puppies for a long time, usually not reaching maturity until after two years of age. Even after that, they retain a mischievous streak that can sometimes get them into trouble. Some Airedales also exhibit considerable aggression toward other dogs, and prospective owners must be willing to socialize and train their terriers to curb this tendency.

Are you prepared to put up with an Airedale's rowdiness, unique personality, and disruptive antics? More than one Airedale has interrupted a human social gathering to display something fragrant it has just dug up or rolled in, or to show off a dead rodent it was just dying to share. An Airedale can carry an amazing amount of dirt, mud, and burrs in its furnishings or an equally amazing amount of water in its beard just after getting a nice drink. Unfortunately, it's at times like these that an Airedale seems to be particularly desirous of human company and affection!

Airedale puppies are a handful. They have an almost limitless supply of energy and are into something most of the time they are awake. It often seems that the only time they are quiet is when they are asleep. Destructive chewing can be a major problem with young Airedales. It may surprise a new Airedale owner just how quickly furniture can be dismantled if a puppy is left to entertain itself. They are also notorious diggers, and can quickly turn the most elegant landscaping into something resembling Swiss cheese. Most Airedales also have the typically terrier trait of barking at anything they notice, and they notice everything. Squirrels, passing dogs, or pedestrians, and sometimes even clouds and airplanes must be commented on or warned off. In spite of these less than desirable traits, however, Airedales are very trainable. They are also smart enough to realize when they must turn on the charm. They do grow up eventually and are wonderfully devoted, protective, bright, and entertaining companions.

Airedales can make wonderful pals for considerate children. They are active and playful, and not particularly delicate. They are strong and forceful, however, and play sessions should be monitored by an adult. Young Airedales may not be the ideal playmate for toddlers as their rough-and-tumble play may result in the child's being knocked off its feet, but, with adult supervision, an Airedale can be a child's best buddy.

The Airedale is a high-maintenance breed. The lovely crisp black and tan coat seen on the show dog is the product of countless hours of plucking, stripping, and grooming. Most pet Airedales are clipped to keep the coat under control, but there is still a fair amount of combing, brushing, and trimming needed to keep the coat in good condition. Left to its own devices the Airedale's coat will grow to the point that the dog will resemble an animated tumbleweed.

Airedales are not good impulse purchases. Buyers must be aware that they are going to be responsible for a living creature with real needs for possibly more than 13 or 14 years. Therefore, consider your lifestyle and your ability to train and care for a dog before jumping into the role of Airedale owner.

An Airedale in full coat may soon resemble an animated tumbleweed.

Puppy or Adult?

A puppy can be taught from the start what behavior will be appreciated and what won't be tolerated. Young Airedale puppies are fairly easy to housebreak and learn basic household obedience commands quickly. Early, consistent training is a necessity for such a high-spirited breed. An Airedale puppy can be taught from the start to accept other family pets. Airedales raised from the beginning with other dogs will accept them as part of the family, and they must be carefully socialized with dogs outside the family circle to avoid problems later on. Thoughtfully trained and raised with love and care, an Airedale that is acquired as a puppy can become a truly "customized" family pet.

Adopting an adult Airedale is also an option worthy of consideration. Older dogs that have already received training usually have already outgrown puppy mischief. They are often housebroken and may be a bit calmer than pups. Adopting an older Airedale is often a better choice for people who work full time, senior citizens, and people who don't have the time or patience to work with an energetic puppy.

Male or Female?

Is a male or female the better pet? That is strictly a matter of preference. Females eventually go into season, during which time they must be kept closely guarded lest they be bred by one of the many amorous male dogs that will show up in the front yard. I strongly recommend spaying females unless they are to be bred. Spayed females generally get along with other dogs, although this is not always the rule. Males are bigger and stronger, and sometimes are more aggressive to other dogs. On the flip side, however, males can be just as sweet and devoted to their family as females. Both sexes are protective of their families.

Airedales as Gifts

If you're considering giving an Airedale as a gift, give thought to whether the recipient really wants the responsibility of a dog. Even the cutest baby Airedale will be much less

Airedales can be wonderful companions for considerate children.

than cute after it has shredded a chair, had an encounter with a skunk, gotten into a fight, or caused a visit from the police because of an evening of barking. As it grows into adulthood, it will appear less than wonderful if the

An observant breeder will know which is the best pup for a prospective buyer.

recipient doesn't have the time for the training, exercise, and grooming the breed requires.

How to Find Your Airedale Terrier

If you decide on a puppy, my best advice is to buy your Airedale from a reputable breeder who will allow you to meet the puppy's mother and to visit it in its original home. Most breeders do not own both parents, but they should still be able to provide good information about the sire. A list of breeders may be obtained from the Airedale Terrier Club of America, or the various regional Airedale clubs (see page 91 for addresses). Newspaper classified ads will occasionally list Airedales for sale, but this is not the best way to find a dog.

Make sure that the sire and dam of the litter are dogs you would like to own yourself, since the puppies will have inherited many of their characteristics. The puppies should be healthy, clean, and friendly, and the nursery should be reasonably clean and odor-free. The breeder should be willing to discuss the health records of the puppies and be forthright with any questions on the health and temperament of the parents. An observant breeder should be able to give you information on each individual puppy's personality. Many good breeders will not allow the prospective buyer to choose his or her own puppy. The breeder will know which is the best bet for a particular situation based on observation of the litter. He or she may have even run puppy aptitude tests on the litter. These are tests that can give an insight into the temperamental makeup of each individual puppy and its suitability for certain types of work. These tests can also help to aid the breeder in making successful matches of puppies to new homes. Rely on the breeder's expertise in making your choice.

Many conscientious breeders offer a contract guaranteeing the health and temperament of their pups and will offer (and usually insist) to take the dog back at any time if the new owner cannot keep it.

A word of caution when you go to visit the breeder: It is very easy to transmit disease to a litter. Make sure you haven't visited another litter the same day, or petted or played with dogs that are not part of your own family. The breeder may ask you to remove your shoes and wash your hands before handling the puppies. Diseases such as parvovirus (see page 41) are extremely contagious and can be fatal to young puppies that have little immunity. Breeders will often appear fanatic about cleanliness around a young litter. Don't interpret this as a slur on your own hygiene, but as a sign of a breeder who truly cares about his or her pups.

Breeders may sometimes also have older puppies or adults in need of homes. A dog they had previously placed may have been returned because of its owner's death, divorce, poor health, or financial circum-stances. An older puppy may have been a show hopeful that didn't mature into championship material. Sometimes a breeder will place a dog that has retired from the show ring rather than have the dog live out its days in a kennel run.

Breed Rescue Services

Older Airedales are also available through breed rescue services. The Airedale Terrier Club of America and most regional Airedale clubs provide rescue services for Airedales in need of re-homing. Some may be trained, sociable, and healthy. Often, however, these are dogs that were picked up as strays or as surrenders by the local animal control service and turned over to the club for placement. Some may

Airedales can be taught to accept other dogs as part of the family.

have been injured, in poor health, neglected, or abused. Some may have had no training. Much work is put into their rehabilitation by dedicated foster families who bring the dogs back to good health, groom them, train them,

Older dogs can be a better choice than puppies for some people.

and then work to place them in loving, permanent homes. Even though some may need extra attention and effort, adopting a rescued Airedale can be a rewarding experience. These dogs usually bond to their new owners quickly and become supremely devoted companions. Their owners also have the satisfaction of knowing they helped save a dog from circumstances it didn't deserve and from possible euthanasia.

Which Dog Is Right for You?

Finding the right Airedale is a matter of choice. First, what will you expect from the dog? If you are an active person, a sound, athletic dog will be a better running companion than a couch potato. Do you want a dog that will play fetch for hours? Find the Airedale with a strong retrieve instinct. Are there young, active children in the family? If so, it will be important to find an easygoing, playful pup or adult that isn't too sensitive to pain or discomfort (in case it is inadvertently stepped on or tripped over.) Do you lead a quiet life and like it that way? The Airedale that seems a bit reserved may be the one for you and you might consider adopting an older dog. Do you want to show a dog in conformation, obedience, or agility? Will it be a hunting companion? Look for a dog with the physical and mental traits and abilities that will help it excel in these fields.

If you are adopting an adult, spend some time alone with the dog if possible. Is it responsive to you? Is it bold, fearful, or aggressive? Question the owner about temperament quirks. How is it around dogs it knows? How does it react to strange dogs? What is its reaction to other animals such as cats? Is the dog a problem barker? How well does it accept grooming? Is it destructive? How is this dog around other people, singly and in groups? Does it have a particular problem with men? Or women? Or children? How is it in the car? How is its health? Does the dog have allergies to food, fleas, dust, pollen? If the dog has had training, ask the owner to demonstrate its skills. Does it respond to a command fairly quickly? Is its response willing and happy, or does the dog seem cowed or fearful?

Will the owners allow you to take the dog "on approval?" If you find after a week or two that you can't handle the dog, can you return it? (Remember, though, the adjustment period may take a while.) Most rescue organizations and breeders will insist that you sign a contract agreeing that you will return the dog if you ever decide you can no longer keep it.

Raising an Airedale Puppy

Preparing Your Home and Yard

I strongly recommend that you allow your new Airedale to be both a house and yard dog, and puppy-proofing both areas will be necessary to avoid trouble.

Pens, Gates, and Crates

You will need to prepare an indoor area where the puppy can be safely confined when it can't be watched. A portable exercise pen allows the puppy to be confined while still providing play space and room for its bed. A crate is also a wise investment. You might shudder at the thought of "caging" your pet, but when a puppy is properly introduced to a crate, it will have a comfortable den in which it can relax. You can also relax while the pup is crated, since it is not likely to get into trouble while confined! (For more on crates, See pages 22–23.)

A portable puppy gate will also be handy. You can find models to fit most doorways; they are readily movable, and they allow a puppy to see into or out of a room. A suitable puppy gate will be constructed entirely of metal or of plastic-coated wire mesh in a wooden frame.

Exercise pens, puppy gates, and crates can be purchased at dog shows, pet supply stores, and from catalogs.

Toys

Collect a variety of toys in various sizes and textures for your puppy. Make sure these are durable and large enough so they cannot be chewed apart and swallowed. Airedale puppies have powerful jaws and most will try their hardest to demolish anything that fits in their mouths.

• High-quality nylon bones and toys are recommended.

• Hard rubber toys can also be good, but watch to see that your puppy hasn't found a way to bite bits off.

• Stuffed toys that squeak are appealing to Airedales of any age, as are the various rope toys. These need to be checked frequently, however, as Airedales quickly disembowel the stuffed toys and shred the ropes.

• Tennis balls are good, but watch that your puppy doesn't skin them (a favorite Airedale activity). Once the fabric skin is removed it is easy for the pup to chew the ball into pieces.

• Dogs also find the toy called the Buster Cube™ engrossing. Place several bits of kibble inside and the puppy will occupy its time with trying to get the goodies out.

A wire crate can be your Airedale's own "den."

Make sure toys cannot easily be chewed apart.

• Small rawhide chew sticks may be given to the youngster on occasion. Purchase rawhide that has been processed in the United States, since most other countries have no real control over the harmful chemicals sometimes used to treat the hides. Larger rawhide products are not the best choice for Airedales as, after a while, the hide becomes soft and pliable. Knotted ends can be untied, chewed off, and swallowed by an Airedale. If a dog swallows a large enough piece it can become lodged in the esophagus or elsewhere, rapidly bringing on an emergency requiring surgery. Similar cautions apply to bones. If you give the pup a bone, make sure it is a large beef knuckle or leg bone and monitor the pup's chewing as bones can splinter and cause major harm. Even if the puppy simply grinds down the knuckle ends into small pieces, swallowing enough of this matter can cause an obstruction and a veterinary emergency.

• Pig ears, chew hooves, and similar treats can be offered, but these should be given in moderation as they can upset digestion if offered too frequently. You won't want your Airedale to chew these items on a prized carpet; the residue can be quite sticky.

The Home

Airedale puppies are famous for their curiosity. They will consider anything within 3 or 4 feet (91–122 cm) off the floor to be fair game, so it might be best to move the knick-knacks and Granny's heirloom crocheted doilies out of reach or into a room that will be off-limits.

House Plants

Make sure house plants within reach of your Airedale are not poisonous. On this page is a partial list of poisonous house plants, some of which can be fatal. (These are marked with an asterisk.) Symptoms of poisoning may include drooling, vomiting, diarrhea, labored breathing, rapid pulse, irregular heartbeat, swelling around the mouth, or difficulty breathing.

Household Products

Hazardous household products must be kept safely out of reach. If the puppy will have access to the garage, pay attention to what is stored there as well. Some hazardous common household substances are listed below. Many can be fatal, even in small doses.
• automotive products—oil, gasoline, antifreeze (ethylene glycol)
• cosmetics, nail polish, polish remover
• detergents, cleansers
• drain cleaners
• fertilizers
• garbage
• herbicides
• household cleaners
• insecticides, snail and slug bait
• paint, paint thinner, brush cleaner

Poisonous House Plants
Amaryllis
Asparagus Fern
Bird of Paradise
*Castor Bean
Jerusalem Cherry
Creeping Charlie
Crown of Thorns
*Dieffenbachia (Dumb Cane)
*Easter Lily
Ivy
*Lily of the Valley
*Mistletoe
*Philodendron
Poinsettia (*Leaves)
Spider Chrysanthemum
Umbrella Plant

• putty
• rodent killers
Electrical cords are another potential hazard. Move any appliance or lamp with a cord the pup can easily reach, or barricade it so it can't be played with. Cords can also be sprayed with a chewing deterrent product such as "Bitter Apple."

A dog door from the house to the outdoors can provide your Airedale with the best of both worlds.

HOW-TO:
Early Puppy Training

Young Airedale puppies are bright, eager, and quick to learn. They will surprise you with their aptitude. An eight-week-old puppy is not too young to begin learning basic obedience. The key to training puppies is to avoid force and to keep it fun. Airedale puppies have short attention spans, so lessons should be kept brief.

"Sit"

To teach your puppy to sit, hold a treat just in front of its mouth, letting the pup nibble a bit if he wants. Tell the puppy, *"Marty, sit"* and slowly bring the treat up a little bit over his head and slightly toward his rear, keeping your hand fairly close to his muzzle. As he follows this motion, he'll sit. That's the moment to give him the treat and praise him enthusiastically. If he stands or jumps to get the treat

Teach your puppy to stand on command by bringing the treat up and out, parallel to the floor.

instead of sitting, you may have raised it too high. Soon he'll sit on command with either the word or the movement of your hand (which has now become a hand signal command.)

"Down"

Teach the *down* in a similar manner. It is easiest to start

Praising enthusiastically while running backwards a few steps will help encourage your puppy to come when it is called.

with a sitting pup. Show him the treat and give the command *"Marty, down."* Slowly bring the treat straight down to the floor between his front legs. As he lowers his front end to get the treat, slowly pull it away from him along the floor. When he sinks into the down position, give it to him and pour on the praise. Repetition will teach him to lie down on command.

"Stand"

Teaching a pup to stand is just as simple. Show him the treat and give the command *"Marty, stand."* Bring the treat up and out, parallel to the ground and on a level with his nose until he's standing. As soon as he's standing, give him the treat and praise him.

"Stay"

Teach the puppy to remain in the sit, down, or stand position by telling him to stay and briefly

Teach your puppy to sit by raising the treat just a bit over its head, and slightly toward its rear.

showing him the palm of your open hand. (This becomes the hand signal for "*Stay*.") If your pup breaks from whatever position you put him in, gently place him back and say, "*No. Stay*." Correct your pup each time he moves out of this position so he understands that he must stay in the position in which you left him. When it's okay for your pup to get up, give a release command like "*Okay, that's all*," and let him get up. Start with five-second stays, and slowly work up to a longer time.

"Come"

Teach the puppy to come on command using the same lure technique. Go up to him, show him the treat, and give the command "*Marty, come*." Run backwards a few steps when he comes for the treat. Praise him enthusiastically as he runs to you. This technique is particularly helpful when your puppy is distracted or occupied with some toy or another dog but the lure may not be necessary at all if the pup is focused on you. Gradually increase the distance between you and your puppy when you call him. If he hesitates, squat or sit on the ground, spread your arms wide, and coax him to you. You look much more inviting in this position. Through repetition your puppy will learn to come as soon as you call him since he gets so much praise and petting from you when he does. A word of caution here: Don't ever call the puppy to you to punish or reprimand him. If you do, the pup will be less likely to come the next time you call.

Teach your puppy to lie down by slowly moving the treat down to the floor, slightly behind its front legs, and then pulling it away until the puppy lies down.

Walking on a Leash

Teaching a young puppy to walk on a leash is not difficult. Snap the leash onto the puppy's collar and let the pup drag it around for a few minutes. Then pick up the end and follow the puppy around. When the youngster is accustomed to this, it's time to teach it to walk with you. Show your puppy a treat and coax it along by having the pup follow it for a few steps as you walk. Stop, praise your puppy, and give it the treat. Gradually increase the distance between treats.

Treats

The primary use of treats in very early puppy training is as a lure to get the puppy to move into a desired position. Once the puppy learns the behavior, food should be given only intermittently, but praise the puppy every time it performs correctly. Your goal should be to discontinue the use of food completely and rely on praise as the sole reward as soon as possible. You will not always have treats with you when you want your Airedale to behave, but you will always be able to praise it. The training in this chapter is intended for puppies from eight weeks to approximately five months of age. After that, you will find that your puppy will have discovered the rest of the world and will be much less focused on you. Puppies from this age through adulthood usually need to be trained with the methods outlined in Training Your Airedale, beginning on page 53.

The Yard

Puppy-proof your yard prior to your Airedale's arrival. Puppies enjoy chewing on branches, roots, and flowers. Make sure any planting in the puppy's area is nonpoisonous. On this page is a partial list of poisonous outdoor plants. These can cause the same problems as poisonous indoor plants. (Those that can be fatal are marked with an asterisk.)

Yard Enclosures

While your Airedale is a puppy—and possibly longer—it is best not to use your entire yard as its confinement area; it is much easier to puppy-proof a smaller area. Meter readers or gardeners may inadvertently leave a gate open, allowing your pup to escape. Airedales also frequently amuse themselves with major excavation projects while in search of real or imaginary critters, leaving your yard resembling the craters of the moon. A dog run or large outdoor kennel can be convenient for confining the puppy when it can't be watched outdoors. Make sure the enclosure is fenced to at least 6 feet (1.8 m) in height. Pouring a concrete strip around the fenced perimeter extending a bit inside and outside will prevent the dog from digging under the enclosure. Or surface the entire run or kennel with concrete. The enclosure should be at least partly shaded and protected from weather extremes. When considering locations, keep in mind that if it is located along a property line fence, activities on the other side may entice the puppy into barking or exhibiting other behavior that may annoy neighbors. Make sure the puppy has a comfortable, weatherproof bed in its enclosure. Your pup will appreciate a place to nap and rest. Provide a variety of interesting playthings. Older puppies and adults may even appreciate a child's wading pool in hot weather.

When your Airedale is a bit older, consider installing a dog door, providing passage between the house and a secure dog run or yard. This provides your Airedale with the best of both worlds.

Airedale puppies can make short work of your garden!

Poisonous Outdoor Plants

Almond	Hemlock
Amaryllis	Ivy
Apricots	Jasmine
*Arrowgrass	Larkspur
Azalea	*Lily of the Valley
Bird of Paradise	Locoweed
*Bittersweet	Lupine
Black Locust	Mock Orange
Buttercup	*Mushroom
*Castor Bean	*Oleander
Cherry Tree	Peach Tree
Crown of Thorns	*Rhubarb
*Daffodil	Skunk Cabbage
Delphinium	*Toadstools
Elderberry	Tomato Vine
Elephant Ears	Wisteria
English Holly	Yew
Foxglove	

Leashes, Collars, and Tags

You will also need a six-foot leather or fabric leash, a soft buckle or quick-snap collar, and an identification tag for the youngster. Airedale puppies are fast and wiggly, and it only takes an instant to slip out of the house or yard. Putting the collar and tag on the pup as soon as you get it can prevent a tragedy. You can even have your dog microchipped for permanent identification. Most animal shelters and many veterinarians keep scanners that can read the embedded chip and reunite you with a lost dog.

A puppy feels secure when it has its own bed for naps and quiet time.

Food

Purchase a supply of the food the breeder had been feeding. (This can be changed to a brand you prefer if you wish, but it's best to keep the puppy on its original diet for at least the first two weeks, or longer. See Feeding Your Airedale, page 47, for information on changing the puppy's diet.) Stainless steel or heavy crockery dishes are recommended for puppies, since the lighter plastic bowls tend to be treated as interesting chew and toss toys. If you use crockery, make sure the glaze doesn't contain lead.

The First Days at Home

Plan to bring the puppy home when you will have ample time to help it get used to its new surroundings. If you work away from the house, this is a good time to use some vacation time. If the pup is a holiday gift, give the recipient a picture of an Airedale puppy, a leash and collar, toys, books, and videos on the breed and training, but don't bring the pup home during the holiday season. There is too much chaos at this time for a new puppy and far too many opportunities for it to get into trouble; wait until after the holidays when the hubbub has died down. The puppy shouldn't be exposed to extra excitement during its first days at home. Let it get used to its surroundings for a few days before starting the social whirl.

On the big day, carry the puppy from the car to your yard and let it relieve itself. Give the pup a chance to explore and then bring it indoors. Let it get acquainted with its new family and explore its new home. Children should be instructed to leave the puppy alone for a little while and to just quietly greet it. Watch closely for any signs that the pup may need to relieve itself. Catching the youngster just before it has an accident and depositing it outdoors to complete the job will get its housetraining off to a good start. Always heap on the praise when the puppy "goes" outdoors.

The hour or so just before bedtime should be quiet time. Too much rough play will leave the puppy wired, making sleep difficult for all of you. Take the pup outdoors one last time to relieve itself. Crate the puppy or put it in its indoor enclosure with a toy. Expect the youngster to cry the first night or two. A ticking clock or a radio playing soft music at a low volume may help soothe it to sleep. Resist the temptation to go to your puppy every time it whimpers unless it really

A portable puppy gate will be a wise investment.

crates or travel kennels. The wire mesh crate can be folded for storage and provides good ventilation. It can be partially covered with a blanket for privacy. Some wire crates have a disadvantage, though. Puppy feet and jaws can get caught in the wide spaces between the wires of a few brands. Look for a model with relatively small spacing between the wires, making the trapping hazard unlikely. The other type to consider is the high-density plastic travel crate. These offer the puppy more privacy than an uncovered wire crate, but care must be taken to provide sufficient ventilation. The door can be removed, leaving the crate usable as a doghouse or an indoor hideaway. A properly sized crate will be big enough for a dog to comfortably lie down, stand up, turn around, and sit.

A word of caution on the use of crates: They should not be used regularly for long-term confinement of a dog, except for overnight use. Don't rely on a crate as a substitute for training a dog to behave. You'll find crates extremely useful in the following situations:

• housebreaking
• confining the destructive chewer when it can't be watched
• confining a sick or injured pet
• traveling (canine equivalent of the seat belt)
• visiting friends and family
• providing the pup with a safe haven when it's upset by children, non-dog-loving guests, fireworks, or trick-or-treaters

If your puppy hasn't been introduced to crates by its breeder, you will need to teach it. Crate training is quite easy and shouldn't take too long. Arm yourself with a pocketful of treats and a crate furnished with a comfortable bed and a toy. Let the puppy investigate, and if it goes inside to explore, praise the pup for its bravery and give

sounds distressed. Give the pup a chance to settle down on its own.

If your puppy wakes you in the middle of the night after initially settling down, it may need to relieve itself. If the pup repeatedly gets you up in the middle of the night, and it isn't sick, it's probably learned a valuable lesson—make enough of a fuss, whether you need to or not, and your human will come.

Confining the Puppy

Crates

Unless you are prepared to follow your pup around 24 hours a day, you must teach it to accept confinement. This process began when you started leaving it alone at bedtime, a relatively easy time for it to accept solitude. What is more difficult is accustoming it to being confined during the daytime. When a puppy needs to be left for only a short period—such as a few hours—a crate is ideal. There are two types to consider: collapsible wire it a treat. If it's hesitant, toss a treat inside. You may need to coax or place your puppy inside the first few times, but reward it every time. Add a phrase like "Go to bed" when your pup gets into the crate or you place it inside. When the puppy seems content inside, close the door. Then open it right away and quietly praise the pup. The next time, leave it in the closed crate a bit longer. Finally, put your puppy in the crate and walk away. If the pup whines or barks a bit when you close the crate door, try to ignore it. Unless it's throwing a tantrum or sounds panicked, it's best not to return right away or you will be teaching your puppy that it can get you back by merely carrying on. Feeding your puppy inside its crate, with or without closing the door, is also a good way to accustom the pup to it.

Some people advocate removing the dog's collar when it is in its crate. A crated dog (or any unattended dog) should never be wearing a choke or slip collar. There have been instances where the "live" ring of one of these has caught on part of the crate and strangled the dog. A buckle or snap collar should not present this problem, but you may want to remove the collar until the puppy has learned to stay in its crate without fussing.

Exercise Pens

Consider using an exercise pen to confine your puppy for longer periods. These are portable enclosures made of wire panels that connect to each other, forming a small corral. Put the puppy's crate or bed and its food and water dishes inside, provide some toys, and you have an easy way to keep the pup out of trouble when you can't watch it.

If your puppy protests confinement, barking or howling excessively, give thought to your actions when you leave and return. Dramatic departure scenes

An exercise pen will keep your pup safely confined when it can't be watched.

provide perfect setups for separation anxiety. Confine your pup 15 minutes or so before you leave. Quietly tell it to be a good puppy and walk away. Come back if necessary to correct tantrums, but keep everything as low-key as possible. When you return, calmly let the pup out and act like you never left. Your departures and arrivals will soon become less stressful.

Housetraining

Airedale puppies aren't difficult to housetrain—all it takes is vigilance, eyes in back of your head, and a great sense of timing. A truckload of paper towels will help, too. Decide where you want your Airedale to relieve itself. Then, any time your pup uses this area, praise it. A very young puppy will need to be taken out every two hours while it is awake. It will need to urinate as soon as it wakes up and after play sessions. It will need to defecate shortly after eating. Make sure the pup has been taken out just before bedtime. Watch for signs that the puppy is getting ready to eliminate indoors or in another off-limits area. It may begin to do a lot of sniffing. It may just look squirmy. The start of a squat is a sure

A crate is a wise investment.

sign. While your Airedale is very young, you will have to quickly scoop the pup up and deposit it in its bathroom area. Add a command word or phrase with the act of urination or defecation. Just as the pup begins to relieve itself say something like "*Good puppy. Go potty*" or "*Do your business.*" Your pup will eventually learn to relieve itself on command this way. As it grows, the puppy will be able to restrain itself while you scoot it out the door under its own power. It will eventually tell you in some way that it needs to go, and then you'll know you have just about won the battle. The pup may bark, whine, or scratch at the door. And you can easily teach your dog to hit a bell hanging from a cord on the doorknob to alert you.

Accidents

Rubbing your puppy's nose in an accidental mess or hitting it with a newspaper won't encourage housetraining. Just resign yourself to cleaning up and watching it more closely next time. Be careful how you clean up indoor accidents. Simply wiping up liquid or scooping up solids isn't enough. Even soap and water may not be sufficient. Wash the area thoroughly, and follow up with the application of an enzyme product like Nature's Miracle, Outright Simple Solution, or Odormute. Without a thorough cleanup and deodorizing, your dog may still be able to detect the scent of urine even though you can't smell it yourself. Since dogs tend to urinate in an area they have used before, if your puppy can still detect the odor, it will probably try that spot again.

The Crate in Housetraining

How do you handle housetraining overnight? This is a good time for the crate. It's natural for a dog to try to avoid soiling its den, and if your puppy's been crate-trained it will consider the crate its den. We can take advantage of this instinct to teach a dog to be clean indoors. Make sure your puppy has a chance to relieve itself before bedtime. Don't simply assume it's done its business; stand there and wait until it does and praise the pup. If you have an adult-size crate for your puppy you may find that temporarily partitioning it so that the floor area is smaller will help to encourage cleanliness. If the pup is able to relieve itself at one end and use the opposite end for its bed, the crate will not be particularly helpful as a housebreaking aid. This natural inclination to keep its den clean can be defeated if you leave the puppy crated so long that it has no choice but to soil it.

Newspapers

How do you handle housetraining indoors when you are not able to watch the pup and a crate isn't practical? Confine the youngster in an exercise pen or other enclosure and cover the floor with newspapers. At first you will be papering the entire area. Once the puppy has established its bathroom spot you can reduce the papered area. Gradually decrease the covered area as long as the pup soils only on the papers. If the puppy begins soiling the floor instead of the papers, increase coverage.

Be realistic in your expectations. Puppies can only be expected to hold it for a reasonable amount of time, and accidents must be expected. No pup should be expected to stay clean

A very young puppy will need to be taken out to relieve itself every two hours while it is awake.

and dry all day while its owner is off at work for nine or ten hours.

Illness

Housetraining can be delayed by illness. If you are having unusual difficulty housetraining, or if it seems as if the pup is constantly having to urinate, take it to the veterinarian for a checkup. A bladder infection may be the culprit. If the puppy has diarrhea it will have problems controlling its bowels. Take the pup out more frequently, and when you can't keep an eye on it confine the pup in the pen with a good supply of newspapers. Don't hold the puppy responsible for accidents when it is ill.

Cleaning Up

Pick up feces from the yard frequently. Besides the obvious odor and fly problem, bored puppies occasionally get into the habit of eating them. A common misconception is that dogs only eat feces if they are missing a vital nutrient from their diet. This is certainly a valid reason, but if you are feeding a quality food in adequate amounts, it is probably not why your pup is ingesting its own waste. Some dogs simply develop a taste for this, revolting as it seems. The best solution is to pick up waste as soon as it is deposited. If your puppy does develop disgusting this habit there are food additives your veterinarian can recommend that may help break this unpleasant practice.

Puppy Nutrition

An Airedale puppy needs a high-quality diet while it is growing. Basic nutritional information is presented in Feeding Your Airedale, beginning on page 47. Most people feed a specially formulated commercial puppy food for the first six to twelve months and then switch to an adult maintenance diet. Don't overfeed the puppy. Recent studies link the overfeeding of higher protein puppy food with poor joint development, particularly the hips. Resist the temptation to supplement a puppy's diet with extra calcium or other additives unless your veterinarian has recommended it.

Young puppies from eight to twelve weeks of age need four meals a day. Keeping the evening meal small will aid housetraining. From twelve weeks through six months a puppy needs three meals a day. After six months and up to a year, your Airedale needs two meals a day. Adult Airedales require only one meal a day, but many people find it preferable to keep the dog on two meals for life.

Fresh water must always be available. Water may be withheld an hour or two before bedtime and during the night if the dog is having difficulty getting through the night without urinating.

Puppy Health Care

Introduce your puppy to its veterinarian a day or two after bringing it home. The doctor will give the youngster a thorough examination and will recommend a vaccination schedule.

Your puppy probably received its first shots while it was still with the breeder, usually from six to eight weeks of age. Your veterinarian will repeat these inoculations at ten to twelve weeks, and then again at fourteen to sixteen weeks. (Some veterinarians will vary this schedule somewhat; follow his or her advice.) The puppy will be vaccinated against distemper, hepatitis, leptospirosis, parvovirus, parainfluenza, and coronavirus. These inoculations are repeated yearly once the puppy series is completed.

When puppies are very young, before they have finished their puppy vaccinations, they are very susceptible to contagious diseases. Diseases that are serious, but treatable, in adult dogs can be fatal to young puppies. Parvovirus and coronavirus are two particular examples. For its safety, keep your puppy home until it has received its permanent inoculations. You will be tempted to take your pup out to show it off, but you will be taking a terrible risk if you do so.

Your puppy will receive its first rabies vaccination at about 16 weeks. It will receive the second a year later, and subsequent rabies shots will be on a two- or three-year schedule as recommended by your veterinarian.

Internal parasites (worms) can also be present in puppies. Bring a fecal sample for analysis when you first take your pup for an examination and at regular intervals throughout its life. These are best treated under a veterinarian's supervision and not with over-the-counter remedies.

Common sense and care will prevent most catastrophes while your puppy is growing up. Health matters are further discussed in Health Care for the Airedale Terrier in the chapter that follows.

Handling Your Airedale

Your puppy training curriculum should include getting your Airedale accustomed to being handled. Your dog will spend a lot of its life being groomed, and both you and your veterinarian will need to be able to examine it. You can make physical handling a pleasant experience by conditioning your puppy to accept handling while very young. Keep your movements slow and talk soothingly to it during these lessons. Begin by handling the pup's legs and feet. Gently touch and hold each of its toes, paying special attention to the toenails. Praise and treat it again. Continue by conditioning your pup to accept having its ears handled inside and out. Teach it to let you gently hold its muzzle. Lift the pup's lip and run your index finger over its teeth. If your puppy attempts to snap or chew on you at any time, lightly squeeze its muzzle with your hand and tell it, "*No biting.*" Gently pull a bit on the pup's ears and tail, rewarding it with a treat for accepting this behavior. Playfully slap or tap (lightly, please) at its sides and give it another treat. Keep sessions short, gentle, and pleasant in order to make grooming and examinations much less of a rodeo.

Training and Socialization

As soon as your Airedale has finished its puppy vaccinations, enroll it in a puppy training class. (These are also called Puppy Kindergarten or Puppy Socialization classes.) Your puppy will learn to mind you when it would rather be playing, it will learn to behave around other people, and it will have a chance to socialize with other puppies. If you are lucky enough to enroll in a class with young children in attendance, your dog will get valuable early exposure to children. These classes are very important for a breed that can be a bit "sharp" without early socialization with other dogs. A knowledgeable instructor can spot potential problems such as aggression or shyness and help you prevent these from becoming major issues later. You will find puppy classes a great deal of fun for both you and your Airedale. An added bonus is that your pup will come home exhausted and will sleep soundly! Any early puppy training class you attend should be based primarily on no-force training, using food, praise, toys, clickers, or similar reinforcements in a positive training program. Avoid classes that rely heavily on physical correction, as these are

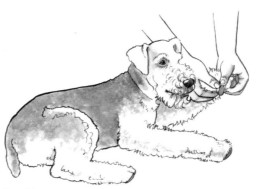

Condition your puppy to enjoy being handled. Pay special attention to handling the feet, toes, and nails.

Consider the possible consequences of anything you allow your puppy to do.

be better to stop it in the act. And what could be more adorable than an Airedale puppy cocking its head and lifting a paw as it gazes at your hamburger? Give it a bite now and you're asking for begging problems in the future. The key to avoiding many bad habits is obvious—don't let the puppy ever start. A few others may need some training to eliminate.

Getting on the Furniture

Consider the problem of an Airedale on the furniture. It's easy to order the dog down when you're at home, but how do you deal with this when you are away? One obvious method is confinement. There are also products on the market that help teach a dog to stay off furniture. One of these is a plastic mat with a battery-operated sensor. Any pressure or movement causes a high whistle to be emitted as long as the pressure continues. There is also is a palm-sized device that works on the same principle. It can be placed on something you want your Airedale to stay off and the slightest jiggle will set off a squeal. Dog supply catalogs carry these items. A strip of wire mesh or one panel of an exercise pen laid across a piece of furniture will also discourage climbing up.

Barking

Puppy barking can be discouraged by distracting the puppy from the object of its concern. Call it, or drop a shaker can on the ground to get its attention elsewhere. You can make a shaker can by putting three or four small stones or marbles in a soda or juice can and taping the hole shut, When the puppy stops, praise it with a comment like "*Good puppy. Be quiet.*" For serious barking problems, try a squirt gun or water spray bottle to stop the pup. If barking or howling is a problem when you aren't home, confine your puppy indoors and leave a radio playing. This

not appropriate for young puppies. A pup will learn in classes like these, but it will resent training.

Avoiding Bad Habits

Anything you start doing with your puppy will have ramifications that last throughout its life. Consider the possible consequences of anything you allow your puppy to do. Will it still seem cute when it's an adult? If you won't want your adult Airedale sleeping on your bed or sitting on your furniture, don't allow it to start doing it as a puppy. You won't want your adult Airedale jumping up on anybody, so don't let it get away with doing so as a puppy. Instead, teach your pup to sit for a greeting. You may think your puppy is cute as can be when it's tearing around the house with your shoe, but will you want it chewing on your things later on? A puppy intent on a major excavation project might be a subject worth grabbing the video camera for, but it would will mask many of the sounds that trigger nuisance barking.

Digging

Digging is a common terrier problem. A puppy that is bored or stressed may seek relief by digging. The hunting instinct can also trigger a digging binge. Some Airedales will dig a hole in which to cool off on a hot day. The shaker can be used to distract a pup that is intent on digging to the center of the earth. Remember to drop the can on the ground or throw it in the vicinity of the pup, but not directly at it. If the puppy keeps going back to the same location to dig, lay a piece of chicken wire in the hole and cover it with an inch or two of dirt. This will discourage the pup. You might also try one of the products designed to repel animals from the area where it has been applied. Consider providing the puppy with a digging pit of its own. Outline a small area of loose dirt or sand and bury a couple of toys in it. Each time you catch your puppy digging, take it over to its own pit and let it dig there. Your Airedale will be able to act on its instincts without ruining your garden.

Mouthing and Biting

Mouthing and biting are problems every Airedale puppy owner has to deal with. This is a normal part of puppy behavior, especially around teething time; it does not necessarily mean that you have an aggressive dog. Correct biting or mouthing with a sharp squeal and a verbal reprimand. If this doesn't work, try a quick shake of the muzzle or the scruff of the neck. If your puppy repeatedly goes back to mouthing, put it in its crate or pen for a time-out. Engaging in games of tug-of-war during this period can send your puppy mixed signals. On one hand you are letting it know that you enjoy having it use the force of its

jaws in a game with you, and on another you are telling it you don't. Roughhousing encourages this type of behavior, so it's best to avoid these games during this period. The pup will soon learn that play or petting sessions end if the behavior continues. This mouthy period may seem to last forever, but Airedales really do grow out of it quickly.

Growling during Eating

Don't allow your puppy to growl at you while it is eating. Accustom it to your touching the bowl, placing your

Don't let nuisance barking become a problem.

Airedale puppies seem to enjoy chewing objects that are strictly off limits.

hand in its food, and occasionally moving the bowl around a bit during a meal. If your puppy attempts to warn you off, take the bowl away for a few moments. One way to teach your puppy to welcome your interference is to interrupt it by putting a small bit of something extra-tasty in its dish while it is eating. This training should be done by an adult, not by children. It is always advisable to teach children to leave the dog alone while it is eating.

Chewing

Destructive chewing is probably the most common problem behavior. Airedales have powerful jaws. Puppies chew to relieve the pain and discomfort of teething. They also chew just for the fun of it. Be vigilant and provide your pup with a variety of things of its own to gnaw. When you catch your Airedale in the act of chewing something forbidden, take it away with a reprimand and give the pup something of its own to chew. If your puppy's developed a taste for table legs, electrical cords, carpet edges, or other items you'd rather it left alone, spray or rub one of the anti-chewing prod-

ucts such as Grannick's Bitter Apple on them. This foul-tasting substance discourages most chewers. Bitter Apple must be reapplied often while the puppy is going through this stage. For the occasional Airedale that actually likes the taste of Bitter Apple, try hot pepper sauce or cayenne pepper. It can be helpful to keep your puppy's available toy supply down to less than a boxcar-load during this period. If it has too many toys out at any one time, it may figure everything in the house is a chew toy. Rotate the toys your pup has out at any time, changing the selection every few days to keep it interesting. One positive aspect of the chewing period is that it helps teach children to pick up and put away their toys, shoes, and socks!

Stealing

Stealing from counters and tabletops is another favorite activity of unsupervised Airedales. Either of the pressure-sensitive sound devices described previously can be placed on these surfaces. Even if the sound doesn't stop the puppy in its tracks, you will be alerted so that you can get to it for a correction. You can also balance shaker cans on the edge, relying on the sound of the falling cans to discourage the behavior. Another method (which sounds worse than it is) is to place a set mousetrap on the surface. (Make sure the trap is a new one, not one that has been used for its original purpose of trapping mice as the lingering scent and germs may cause other problems.) The sound and jump of the snapping trap will convince most puppies that they didn't really want to be up there anyway. You might fear the trap will catch your dog's toes, but I've never seen this happen. If you want to eliminate all chances of snapped toes, try the clever device called the Snappy Trainer. This is a mousetrap with a plastic paddle on the snapper. It snaps just as quickly as a plain trap, but the paddle prevents any chance of injury.

Use Verbal Reprimands

When it is necessary to reprimand a young puppy, it is important to use the mildest one that is effective. A stern verbal reprimand is usually enough. Sometimes the best correction, especially if the little devil goes right back to what it was doing wrong in the first place, is to put the pup in its crate or pen for a short time-out. Swatting a puppy with your hand is rarely appropriate. Hitting a puppy with a rolled-up newspaper or any other object is *never* acceptable.

The Adolescent Airedale

Just when you think you have the perfect puppy—well trained, good social skills, happy, and cooperative— *it* rears its ugly head. What is *it*? Adolescence! All of a sudden your wonderful puppy forgets everything it has learned, it's surly on occasion, and sometimes it ignores you completely. Your Airedale may be starting to get testy around other dogs. It's even urinating in the house again although it was housetrained. What could have gone wrong? Actually, nothing has gone wrong; your pup's just going through the rocky transition between puppyhood and adulthood. It's a teenager! This is the time for patience, firmer discipline, and more obedience training. Provide your Airedale with plenty of exercise so that it can burn off some excess energy. Adolescence is a time of testing. Dogs are pack animals, and if left in an all-dog pack, the adolescents would be jostling with the more dominant adult dogs to move up higher in rank. They will do the same with their human packs. This is also a good time to consider spaying or neutering. These procedures won't lessen your dog's value as a pet and personal guardian, but they may help to alleviate some of the behavior problems associated with raging adolescent hormones. If your male has begun to urinate in the house or other inappropriate places, he is marking his territory. Neutering at this age, along with correcting the dog when you do catch him in the act, can help stop this problem. Neutering also eliminates the possibilities of testicular cancer and reduces the incidence of prostate problems when the dog is older. Spayed bitches are often less moody than intact bitches experiencing hormonal swings, and the obvious problem of attracting every male dog within miles during her heat periods will be eliminated. Also, a bitch who was spayed while she was young will be less likely to suffer from mammary tumors.

Airedales eventually grow out of adolescence, thankfully, usually by the age of two years. Patience, vigilance, training, and reinforcement of good behavior will get you through this period.

Health Care

Finding a Veterinarian

Your main ally in maintaining your Airedale's good health is a veterinarian you like and trust. Finding just the right veterinarian is an important task. If you don't already have one picked out, ask for recommendations. A conscientious breeder doesn't skimp on quality veterinary care, so this can be a good way to make a choice. Check with pet-owning friends and coworkers. Don't choose a veterinarian simply because the clinic is the closest one to your home. It's more important to have a competent veterinarian who operates a clean, well-equipped clinic and with whom you have a good rapport even if this person is a few miles farther away.

If the clinic you have chosen is not open after hours, on weekends, or on holidays, look up the closest veterinary emergency clinic and keep the address and telephone number handy. Airedales have a habit of scheduling emergencies after hours. These clinics are open when regular clinics are closed. They are staffed with veterinarians and technicians who are accustomed to handling emergencies and pets needing their services are transferred to their regular clinics during the day.

Preventive Medicine

Preventive medicine is the foundation of good health. Every Airedale should see its veterinarian at least once a year. This annual check-up will include a physical examination and an update on any booster shots due. The veterinarian may request that you bring a fecal specimen to test for worms, and may draw blood to test for the presence of heartworms. Eyes, ears, and teeth will be examined. The veterinarian will examine the coat and skin for signs of fleas, dermatitis, or other problems. Heartbeat and respiration will be checked. Depending on the age and condition of your Airedale, the veterinarian may recommend additional blood work or other tests.

A major part of preventive medicine is keeping up-to-date on vaccinations. Thanks to widespread inoculation, distemper, leptospirosis, and hepatitis are no longer the common killers they once were and coronavirus, parvovirus, and parainfluenza are less of a problem. Regular rabies vaccinations can prevent that dread disease. Many wild animals that inhabit even urban areas, such as raccoons and bats, can be carriers. Even though your Airedale is current on its rabies vaccination, call your veterinarian if it has been in contact with a possibly infected animal.

Preventive health care does not stop at the veterinarian's clinic. A good deal is done right at home. Grooming day is a good time to perform your own examination. Check the coat and skin for fleas, rashes, hair loss, or dryness. Examine the feet thoroughly for foxtails, burrs, or awns (the slender bristles found in some grasses). Check ears for inflammation, soreness, or excess wax; a foul-smelling ear can be the sign of an infection. Check the mouth. Are the teeth clean, or is it time to schedule a cleaning? Further information on the care of feet, ears and teeth are included in Grooming the Airedale Terrier, beginning on page 64. Check your dog's eyes. Are they clear and bright? Is there a discharge, which can be the symptom of an infection, allergy, or the presence of a foreign body? Run your hands over your dog's body, head, neck, tail and legs. Check for sore spots or swellings. If your Airedale is a senior citizen, check for any lumps or growths that should be brought to the attention of the veterinarian.

Preventive medicine also includes good nutrition. The Airedale should be fed a high-quality diet in clean dishes. Ample amounts of fresh, clean water should be available.

Staying Fit

Adequate exercise is important. Don't make the mistake of assuming your dog gets enough just because you have a large yard. Most dogs won't exercise themselves without some help from you. Airedales benefit from long walks, and two or three miles a day isn't too much for sound, healthy dogs.

Running your dog on leash next to you is an excellent form of exercise. Running should not be done with an Airedale that is less than a year old because of the possibility of damage to the growing dog's joints, cartilage, and tendons. Don't run your Airedale in hot weather, unless you can do it at night or in the very early morning. Not only will *you* risk heat stroke, but some surfaces may burn your dog's feet. Check your Airedale's feet periodically when running.

Fetching Frisbees or tennis balls is a favorite exercise of Airedales and allows them to really stretch their legs, but Airedales were not built for flying jumps and a bad landing can result in back or leg injury so keep your throws low to the ground.

Swimming is wonderful exercise and many Airedales love to swim. Limit rigorous exercise sessions to the coolest parts of the day in warm weather.

Preventive medicine can help keep your Airedale active for many years.

Dog Runs and Parks

Many cities provide enclosed dog runs in their parks. These are fenced areas where dogs are allowed to run and play off leash. They can be a great way to exercise a dog, but they also present a few hazards.

On the plus side, your Airedale will get the chance to play with other dogs, and will be able to run until he's exhausted. Some dog parks are equipped with poop scooper dispensers, trash cans, and water fountains, and are kept clean by responsible dog owners.

On the other hand, your dog may be exposed to aggressive dogs looking for a fight, or he might try to start a fight himself. Public dog runs might not always be scrupulously clean, and your Airedale could be exposed to diseases carried by other dogs.

If your city provides a public dog run or dog park, check it carefully before taking your dog there for a romp. Be sure there are no means of escape through a gap in the fence or a loose gate.

HOW-TO:
Flea and
Tick Control

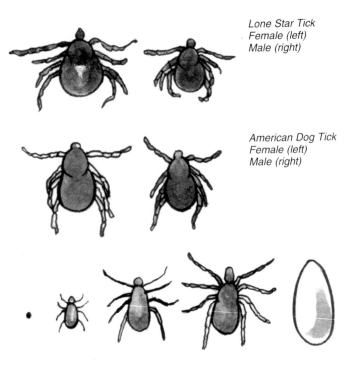

Lone Star Tick
Female (left)
Male (right)

American Dog Tick
Female (left)
Male (right)

Fleas

The most common pest you will encounter is the flea. Flea control is a part-time project in colder climates, but residents of many parts of the country find it a full-time job. Many Airedales are allergic to flea bites, and can have reactions that run from merely uncomfortable all the way to serious. The first line of defense is to treat the dog. There are many good flea-control products on the market. Products containing growth regulators (which prevent flea eggs from hatching as well as killing adult fleas) are particularly useful.

Treating the Environment

You must also treat your pet's environment. Bedding, crates, furniture and carpets, your yard, and possibly even your car, your cottage at the lake, or wherever the dog has spent time will all need to be treated. Several manufacturers package complete flea control management systems that include everything you need to treat your pet and its environment.

Deer Tick
(from left to right) Nymph, Young, Adult Male, Adult Female, Sesame Seed

These usually include a spray or fogger for indoor use, a spray for outdoors, and flea shampoo and/or flea spray for use on the dog.

Reading Labels

Read the labels carefully on any products you use. Don't exceed the amount of spray or the frequency of application listed by the manufacturer. If your Airedale is a puppy, be sure the product is approved for use on puppies. Be particularly careful of using more than one product at the same time. Exposure to a mixture of insecticides can be dangerous. Many products are not intended to be

used in conjunction with other products. Consult your veterinarian for information on the best and safest flea control products to use.

There have been marvelous advances recently in flea control products available through veterinarians. Among the new weapons available are liquids applied monthly to the skin that kill fleas that land on the dog as well as pills given monthly to the dog that prevent fleas from breeding. These products are very effective.

Many "natural" flea control products are also available, and some are fairly effective in mild cases. Many people swear by

Public Enemy Number One: the flea.

brewer's yeast and garlic added to the dog's daily ration. There is no hard evidence that this is actually effective in repelling fleas, but it is safe to use in the recommended doses.

Signs of a Flea Problem

The most obvious sign of a flea problem is a scratching pet. Don't assume that if you can't see fleas your dog doesn't have them. Fleas don't spend all their time hitchhiking on your Airedale; they spend a great deal of their life cycle off the pet as well. Even if you don't actually see fleas, there will be other signs of infestation, such as small specks of flea feces that appear as tiny flakes of blood or dirt on the skin.

Ticks

Ticks are a problem in many areas of the country. Any time you have your Airedale in grassy fields or woodlands, check for these potentially dangerous pests. Once ticks have attached themselves to a dog, they feed on its blood and may swell to the size of a small bean. Ticks can range in size

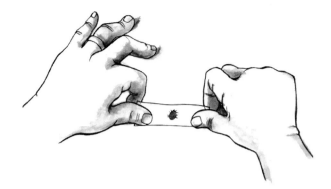

Ticks transmit disease to dogs and humans. After removing a tick, sandwich it between two strips of transparent tape and show it to your veterinarian for identification.

from the tiny deer tick, which is poppy seed size in the nymph stage, to the larger dog ticks.

Removing Ticks

Ticks must be removed carefully, and the entire tick must be removed. Make sure the head and mouth parts have been completely extracted, as an infection may result if any part remains. Tweezers or "tick pullers" are handy for this task. Use a steady, slow pull and after removing the tick, swab the skin with alcohol or antiseptic. (If your dog has been exposed to ticks, there is a good chance that you are also carrying them. Check your own body and clothing thoroughly.) Ticks can carry a number of dangerous diseases, such as Lyme disease, Rocky Mountain spotted fever, tick paralysis, and babesiosis, which causes potentially deadly anemia. Do not use your bare hands to remove ticks.

When to Call the Veterinarian

The following signs are indicative of problems requiring veterinary attention. The list is not complete; therefore, when in doubt, call your veterinarian.

- blood in urine or feces
- staggering, shivering, tremors
- fever
- wheezing
- severe or prolonged diarrhea
- diarrhea with blood or mucus present
- severe or prolonged vomiting; blood present in vomitus
- seizures
- swelling and hives
- loss of appetite
- lethargy, listlessness, or depression
- increased water consumption
- increased urination
- animal bites
- nasal bleeding or discharge
- whimpering or crying when touched
- limping
- abnormal appearance of the eyes
- coughing or sneezing
- cut or torn pads
- repeated head shaking
- foul breath
- constipation
- broken tooth
- incessant scratching

Emergencies

The following emergencies require *immediate* veterinary care:

- any incident involving a dog being hit by an automobile
- heavy bleeding
- possible fractures
- burns
- electric shock
- repeated or continuous seizures
- poisonous snakebite
- poisoning
- eye injuries
- unconsciousness or physical collapse
- inability to urinate
- vomiting lasting more than 24 hours
- choking or labored breathing
- severe allergic reactions
- swallowing a foreign object
- gums and mouth appearing very pale or dark purplish-blue
- heat prostration
- whelping difficulties
- any symptom of bloat (gastric dilatation/volvulus).

Severe pain is grounds for a trip to the veterinarian. Airedales are generally very stoic; therefore, an Airedale exhibiting pain may be in a lot more trouble than it appears. Abdominal pain can be a symptom of bloat, gastric dilatation/volvulus, poisoning, internal injury, intestinal obstruction or peritonitis. Pain in a limb may be symptomatic of a fracture, sprain, or dislocation.

Bloat

Bloat (gastric dilatation/volvulus) is a critical condition that is occasionally seen in Airedales and all large, deep-chested breeds. This is an intensely painful, life-threatening condition. The exact causes are not known, but vigorous exercise closely following a large meal, gulping large amounts of air while eating or drinking, and stress are suspects. The earliest symptom is a very taut stomach. The dog will be uneasy, unable to settle down, and will be in pain. It may salivate and it will attempt to vomit or defecate without being able to produce anything. Shortly, the abdomen will begin to swell. Bloat is caused when the stomach fills with gas and fluid. The stomach can quickly rotate on its axis, guaranteeing that the contents cannot be passed. Blood flow to the stomach wall can cease, causing portions of the organ to die. Other organs can also be affected. The dog will become weak and confused; its heartbeat will become rapid and it can go into shock. If the veterinarian is unable to pass a tube into the stomach, surgery is necessary. Dogs that survive must be treated intensively with medication and fluids, and great care must be taken to prevent a recurrence. Feeding smaller meals twice a day and avoiding strenuous exercise for at least an hour after feeding can help prevent this emergency. Bloat is a grave emergency, and the dog must receive medical care at once!

Emergency First Aid

A little knowledge of emergency first aid is valuable. There are several excellent canine health manuals that include information on first aid, and these should be considered required reading (see Useful Addresses and Literature, page 91).

1. Learn the pressure points (the areas where applied pressure can stop bleeding) on a dog. There are four: the head and neck, the foreleg, the hind leg, and the tail. Pressure applied in these locations or on or next to a wound can help slow blood loss. Cold compresses can slow bleeding from the nose or mouth. Tourniquets are rarely advised; they can cause significant damage by preventing blood circulation.

2. Call your veterinarian or the veterinary emergency clinic at once if you suspect your dog has been poisoned, and follow his or her instructions to the letter. Inducing vomiting is not appropriate for many types of poisons, and may cause more damage as the dog vomits.

3. If you suspect your dog has a fracture, try to lift and carry the dog by picking it up by the chest, allowing the limbs to hang free. If this causes too much movement of the injured limb, transport the dog on a stretcher, dog bed, or piece of plywood. Don't attempt to straighten broken bones. Leave this to your veterinarian.

4. Keep the dog quiet and as free from additional stress as possible while transporting it to the veterinary hospital. An injured dog may bite or

An injured dog may snap or bite out of pain or fright. A temporary muzzle can be fashioned from a scarf or belt.

snap out of pain, so unless a respiratory problem is involved, fashion a temporary muzzle for the dog. This can be made from a belt or scarf run in a figure-eight around and under the muzzle, then crossed over the throat and tied in back of the neck.

5. Heat prostration (heat stroke) can occur in warm weather. This frequently happens when a dog has been left in a closed car parked in the sun or, for that matter, anywhere on a warm day. I recommend not leaving a dog in a car when the weather is sunny or 60°F (15.6°C) or above. Symptoms include heavy panting, thick saliva or foam around the mouth, noisy respiration, very high body temperature and severe stress. Attempt to cool your dog's body off with water or ice, and seek veterinary care without delay.

Artificial Respiration/CPR

Artificial respiration and cardiopulmonary resuscitation can be administered to a dog. To administer artificial respiration, make sure that the mouth is clear. Pull the tongue forward and close the mouth. Press the dog's chest with both hands, repeating approximately every five seconds in a regular

CPR can be administered to an Airedale that has stopped breathing and whose heart has ceased beating.

Home Health Care and First Aid

Keep a canine first aid kit handy. This kit should include:

- gauze pads and rolls
- adhesive tape
- ace bandages
- sterile cotton
- tweezers
- a rectal thermometer
- K-Y or petroleum jelly
- alcohol
- ointment for minor wounds and burns
- ophthalmic drops
- blunt-tipped scissors
- hydrogen peroxide
- activated charcoal
- a medicine syringe
- plastic eyedropper
- over-the-counter remedies for gastrointestinal upsets
- buffered aspirin

Ask your veterinarian's advice regarding proper dosages for the human medications and keep this information with the kit.

Taking the Dog's Temperature

When it is necessary to take your dog's temperature, use a rectal thermometer. (Nobody has been able to teach an Airedale to hold the oral kind under his tongue successfully!) Shake the thermometer down and lubricate the end with a bit of K-Y or petroleum jelly. Lift your Airedale's tail and insert the thermometer at least an inch into the rectum, using a slight twisting motion. Hold it in place for about two minutes. Anything between 100.5 and 102°F (38–38.9°C) is considered normal. Report temperatures above or below this range to your veterinarian. Don't release either the thermometer or the dog during this procedure.

Note: Glass thermometers break easily; digital thermometers are preferable to the glass variety.

manner. If this is not working, you may need to try mouth-to-nose respiration: Make sure the mouth is free of foreign objects and pull the tongue forward. Hold the mouth shut to prevent air from escaping while blowing into the nostrils. The proper rate for blowing into the nose is eight to ten times per minute. CPR may be necessary if your dog's heart has stopped beating. Lay the dog on its right side, slightly elevating the chest a bit with a folded towel placed underneath. Check for obstructions in the mouth and pull the tongue forward. Administer three or four quick breaths using the mouth-to-nose technique. If the heart has not started beating, compress the chest over the heart with the heel of your hand. Do 12 to 15 of these press-and-release compressions. Check again for a heartbeat. If there is none, repeat the sequence. To check your dog's pulse, gently feel around the groin area where the rear leg joins the body until you feel the pulse. It can also be felt on the foreleg just below the elbow, and by gently pressing the rib cage over the heart.

If the dog is choking on an object stuck deep in its airway, lay the dog down on a hard surface, place the palms of both hands just behind the last rib and press down and just a little bit upward three or four times.

Administering Medicine

Administering medication is an easily learned technique. Tablets and capsules can be greased with a bit of butter to make them easier to swallow, or they can be hidden in a treat. If the dog isn't willing to swallow a pill, open its mouth and place the pill back on its tongue. Hold the muzzle up and gently stroke the throat to induce swallowing. Airedales are quite adept at hiding pills in their cheeks and spitting them out as soon as they think you aren't watching, so keep an eye on your dog for a few moments. To administer liquid medication, use a plastic eyedropper or a medicine syringe. Hold your Airedale's muzzle upwards and give the medication through a gap in the teeth, or pouch out the lips at the back of the mouth and administer the liquid through that location. Hold your dog's muzzle up, gently stroking the throat to induce swallowing.

Liquid medication can be given easily by using a syringe.

Bandages

Bandages can be made from gauze rolls or pads, held on by adhesive tape. Wounds should be cleaned before bandaging; bandages and casts should be kept clean and dry. When you change a bandage, examine the wound for any signs of pus or infection.

Convalescing

A convalescing Airedale should be kept quiet, and exercise should be limited. Sometimes your veterinarian will advise crate rest to minimize exertion. Keep your dog warm, clean, and comfortable while it is recovering. Your Airedale may appreciate being kept in an area away from noise and excessive activity. Take care that children do not excite or annoy it. Just like us, dogs need their peace and quiet while convalescing.

A convalescing dog may need to be put on a bland diet. Follow your veterinarian's instructions for feeding. Dogs that are convalescing sometimes need to be coaxed to eat. Add a bit of baby food, low-fat broth, cooked egg, yogurt, or cottage cheese to entice the patient to eat. Feeding several small meals a day may be preferable to one or two normal sized feedings.

Parasites and Pests

External Parasites

In addition to fleas and ticks, mites are another parasite that can plague dogs. These microscopic arachnids can cause a variety of unpleasant conditions, the most well known of which is mange. Demodectic mange (demodicosis) is caused by a population explosion of the canine follicular mite, *demodix canis*. The localized form is usually mild; the generalized form can be very serious. Sarcoptic mange, or canine scabies, is an extremely itchy, contagious condition. Ear mites can also attack dogs, causing pain, discomfort, itching, wax and debris buildup, and infection. These conditions should be treated by a veterinarian.

Internal Parasites

Parasites can be a problem internally as well as externally. Internal parasites include tapeworms, hookworms, roundworms, whipworms, heartworms, giardia, and a host of others.

Tapeworms are usually first noticed when the owner spots what appears to be grains of rice in a fresh stool or in the hair around the anus. The presence of roundworms, hookworms, and whipworms can be verified by the veterinarian by fecal examination. A heavy infestation can cause weight loss, debilitation, and even anemia in the dog.

Heartworm is a potentially deadly parasite transmitted to dogs by some kinds of mosquitoes. Heartworm microfilaria are carried by these mosquitoes and eventually the adult worms make their home in the affected dog's heart. Left untreated, the dog will die of heart failure. Treating heartworm disease is a serious, lengthy, and sometimes fatal procedure, but it's easy to prevent by giving the dog regular doses of heartworm preventive medication. Before starting a dog on this preventive, a blood sample must be examined to be sure that no heartworms are already present. Dogs are kept on the medication throughout the mosquito season. In warmer parts of the country, they must be kept on it year-round, but more and more veterinarians recommend year-round use of heartworm preventive all over the United States.

Giardia and *Coccidia* are protozoan parasites that can infect dogs, most commonly causing diarrhea. Giardia can infect dogs that drink water that has been contaminated by the feces of infected wild animals. Coccidia infect puppies more frequently than adults and appears to be more prevalent in crowded conditions, such as kennels and animal shelters.

Gastrointestinal Upsets

Airedales are likely to suffer from the occasional gastrointestinal upset, partly because they would just as soon snack on a bit of very old, dead bird as on caviar. Upsets can also be caused by stress or a change of food. Symptoms may include flatulence, vomiting, and diarrhea. Mild cases can be treated by putting the dog on a water-only diet for up to 24 hours. If your veterinarian approves, give Kaopectate, Maalox, or Pepto-Bismol until the stool consistency begins to normalize and the stomach settles.

Note: Pepto Bismol will turn the feces black.

Gradually get the dog back to food by feeding a bland diet of plain cooked rice and boiled chicken breast, lean beef, or lamb. Gradually mix your dog's regular ration into this mixture and get it back to its normal diet within two or three days. If the condition lasts more than 24 hours, or the dog seems dehydrated, consult your veterinarian. If the dog is a very young puppy, consult the veterinarian as soon as you notice the problem. If blood is visible in the stool or vomitus, or if excessive

A. Hookworm
B. Whipworm male
C. Whipworm female
D. Roundworm
E. Tapeworm

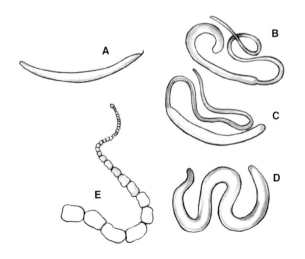

amounts of mucus are present in the stool, consult your veterinarian as soon as the problem occurs.

Viruses

Kennel Cough

Kennel cough (bordatella, canine parainfluenza virus, canine adenovirus, and other viruses) is a highly contagious airborne virus your Airedale may pick up at a boarding kennel, a public dog run, or any place frequented by many dogs. A hoarse cough that becomes more severe with excitement or exercise is the first sign. Kennel cough itself is not a particularly serious disease, but complications and infections such as bronchitis and pneumonia are possible. Contact your veterinarian if your dog shows symptoms.

Canine Parvovirus

Canine parvovirus is another highly contagious disease. Veterinarians vaccinate dogs against this serious illness, but it is still possible for the dog to contract it. Symptoms may include diarrhea, vomiting, high fever, and dehydration. Parvovirus can be rapidly fatal in young puppies. See your veterinarian immediately if you suspect that your dog may have parvovirus.

Other Ailments and Health Problems

Foxtails and Grass Awns

Foxtails and grass awns can cause misery for Airedales. Their thick coats can trap the prickly stickers, which can hide between the toes or pads of the feet. Portions of the stickers can penetrate the skin and travel internally, causing infections. They can enter the ear canal or the eye socket, and they can be inhaled into a dog's nasal passages. Symptoms that the dog may have an inhaled, embedded, or trapped foxtail may include violent sneezing,

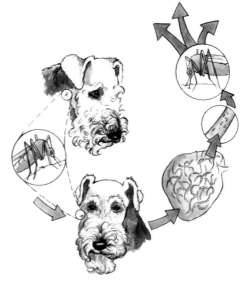

A dog infected with heartworm will die of heart failure if left untreated. This condition can be avoided by administering a daily or monthly dose of heartworm preventive medication.

Airedales will try to eat anything that doesn't eat them first!

repeated head shaking, swelling, or signs of infection in and around the toes and footpads. Keep the ear canal and the area between the toes and pads free of long hair to lessen the chance of a trapped foxtail. Once they have been inhaled, have traveled into the eye socket or deep into the ear, or have penetrated the skin, they must be removed by a veterinarian.

Sprains and Strains

Sprains and muscle strains are fairly common. Swelling can be lessened by placing a cold wrap on the affected area. A dog with a sprain or muscle strain should be kept quiet and inactive. Administering aspirin is usually not advised as the dog will attempt to move about too much if the pain is reduced in this fashion. If lameness persists more than a couple of days or if it increases, take the dog to your veterinarian.

Anal Sac Problems

Anal sac blockage is a bothersome problem that may afflict your Airedale. The anal sacs are small fluid-filled pockets on each side of the dog's

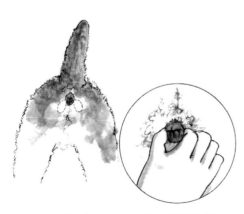

Your Airedale may need assistance in emptying its anal sacs if they become impacted.

anus, slightly below the center line. The fluid normally drains into the rectum, but occasionally the duct that drains them becomes obstructed and can then accumulate and become very uncomfortable. Left untreated, the glands can become infected. Scooting its rump along the floor may be a sign that your dog needs help emptying these glands. This is not difficult, but it isn't a particularly pleasant job as the secretions from anal glands are very foul smelling.

Raise the dog's tail with one hand, and place a cotton pad across the anus with your other hand. Gently grasp the glands between thumb and forefinger. Squeeze lightly while applying upward pressure. You should notice a brownish or yellow thick liquid. If you notice a swollen, abscessed area on either or both sides of the rectum, this is sign of an infection that should be treated by your veterinarian.

Skin Irritations

Hot spots are itchy, painful skin conditions which develop quickly. They are often associated with flea-allergic dermatitis. If you notice a raw, oozing lesion on the skin, schedule an appointment with your veterinarian for treatment.

Special Health Concerns of the Airedale

Allergies

Many Airedales have sensitive skin. Dermatitis and eczema are not uncommon and many Airedales are subject to flea allergies.

Food allergies are also seen in Airedales. These may manifest themselves by poor skin and coat, vomiting, diarrhea, flatulence, or even repeated ear infections. Sometimes the solution is as simple as switching to another type of food. See Feeding Your Airedale, page 47, for information on changing your dog's diet. If a change of diet does not seem to help, consult your veterinarian.

Airedales can also be susceptible to other allergies, including sensitivity to pollens and dust. Skin rashes, ear infections, wheezing, licking or chewing on the feet can be symptomatic. Your veterinarian or veterinary dermatologist can help make an allergic dog more comfortable in its environment.

Hypothyroidism

Hypothyroidism is seen in Airedales. Symptoms may include weight gain, lethargy, hair loss, poor coat condition, and darkened skin. This condition is verified by a blood test, and is easily controlled with daily medication.

Hip Dysplasia

Hip dysplasia, a painful and debilitating malformation of the hip joint, also occurs in Airedales. A good joint has the ball of the femur (thighbone) fitting tightly into the socket of the hip. In dogs with hip dysplasia, the socket may be too shallow or the ligaments and muscle may allow too much slackness. Depending on the severity, the dysplastic dog may show pain, gait abnormalities, difficulty in sitting or lying down or in getting up. Severe cases can be remedied by surgical procedures that may include removing the ball joint, rebuilding the hip, or total hip replacement. Dysplastic Airedales should be kept lean, and exercise should be as recommended by the veterinarian. Hip dysplasia is thought to be inherited, but environmental stresses such as overfeeding and too-rapid growth may exacerbate the disease. Your veterinarian can X-ray your Airedale to determine if it is dysplastic, and this diagnosis can be confirmed by evaluation by the Orthopedic Foundation for Animals (OFA) or by Penn-Hip (see Useful Addresses and Literature, page 91).

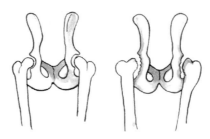

Hip dysplasia can affect Airedales, causing varying degrees of lameness and pain. Left, normal hips. Right, dysplastic hips.

Eye Disorders

Inherited eye disorders occasionally occur in Airedales. Retinal dysplasia and progressive retinal atrophy have been noted in the breed. Other eye disorders that may be hereditary include retinal or corneal dystrophy, pannus, an inflammatory condition of the cornea that can result in blindness, and entropion (inturning eyelids.) Breeders can certify that their stock is free of congenital eye defects through testing by a veterinary ophthalmologist and these certified dogs can be registered with the Canine Eye Registry Foundation (CERF) (see Useful Addresses and Literature, page 91).

Several other diseases and disorders are suspected of being hereditary in Airedales. It is vitally important for breeders to be familiar with these conditions. A conscientious breeder will do all he or she can to prevent them from occurring in puppies. These include:
• Von Willebrand's disease (a blood clotting deficiency)
• cerebellar hypoplasia (underdevelopment of the cerebellum, resulting in incoordination)
• spondylosis deformans (a form of spinal arthritis)
• umbilical hernia (portion of intestine or fatty tissue penetrating the abdominal wall)

- vestibular disorder (causes loss of balance, incoordination)
- lymphosarcoma (a form of cancer)

The Elderly Airedale

Most Airedales stay vigorous well into their teens, but eventually the conditions that plague any senior dog will afflict your Airedale.

Hearing. One of the first problems of increasing age is failing hearing. Often a dog who is losing its hearing can still hear high-pitched sounds, so try raising your voice to a higher pitch, whistling, or clapping your hands to get its attention. It is also helpful to accustom the dog to hand signal commands.

Seeing. The senior Airedale's eyesight will also diminish. You may notice that the dog bumps into objects, or it may have trouble seeing at night, while still getting around well in daylight. You may notice a bluish cast to the eye, which is indicative of failing eyesight.

A dog with failing vision, even a dog that is totally blind, can still get around quite well. It will learn to depend on its memory of the location of obstacles, and its senses of smell and hearing to compensate for the lack of eyesight. Take care not to leave new objects in

Keep your old friend comfortable and supply plenty of ear scratches and love.

your dog's path, and if furniture must be rearranged, make sure the dog is safely guided through the new layout until accustomed to it.

For their own safety, dogs with impaired hearing or vision must be kept on leash unless they are in a safely enclosed area.

Arthritis. Airedales will get achy as they age, just as their human companions do. You may notice that your dog has trouble getting up, especially after a long nap. Older dogs may suffer from arthritis and painful joints. Buffered aspirin can help relieve some of the pain, but discuss this with your veterinarian to avoid problems with the prolonged use of aspirin. Medication that can help restore mobility and relieve pain is also available by prescription.

Incontinence. Incontinence can be a problem for older Airedales and can often be remedied with prescription medications. Older dogs need to be taken outdoors more often to relieve themselves. Don't punish your older Airedale for accidents; the dog has no control over them.

Tumors. Lumps and bumps will show up on your senior dog, and many will be harmless fatty tumors or benign cysts. Unfortunately, older dogs are also prone to malignancies, so it is advisable to have any lump or growth checked by your veterinarian. Any changes to an existing lump should also be reported.

Heart disease. Older dogs are also susceptible to heart disease. Symptoms include fatigue, difficulty breathing, coughing, and a swollen belly. Your veterinarian may prescribe medication and put your dog on a low-fat, low-salt diet. Follow your veterinarian's advice on exercise.

Kidney problems. Kidney disease may eventually rear its ugly head. Watch for increased water intake and increased urination. Older Airedales usually need quite a bit more water than younger ones because their kidneys do not operate as efficiently. Changes in water intake and urine output should be brought to the attention of your veterinarian.

Eating problems. Some Airedales become picky eaters as they age. As the dog's senses of smell and taste weaken, food may be less appealing. A bit of low-sodium, low-fat broth or some canned food added to the ration may help whet your dog's appetite.

Solutions for Caring for the Elderly Dog

Senior dogs still need regular exercise, although rigorous workouts will no longer be appropriate. Slow, leisurely walks will help keep your old fellow limber.

Old dogs are special creatures. Good dogs age like good wine; they become mellower and more valuable as the years go by. Long forgotten is all the mischief they may have gotten into as youngsters. It isn't too much of a sacrifice to make adjustments to accommodate their needs. Your senior citizen will appreciate a cozy bed, a patch of sun to lie in, a little extra warmth on cold nights, and a few extra pats on the head.

Old Airedales are special creatures.

Coping With Death

We would like our Airedales to live as long as we do. Sadly, they don't. All too soon we realize the time has come to say good-bye. It would be wonderful if all dogs could pass away peacefully during their sleep, but that isn't the case for most. The day will come when we realize that life has become very difficult for our old friend. Our Airedale may be so debilitated by pain or disease that life holds no joy for it any more. We have the ability to end our dog's suffering painlessly through euthanasia when its quality of life is no longer what we wish for it. Hard as it is to imagine life without our

Remember the good times you shared with your Airedale.

45

Airedale, it is often kinder to offer the dog a humane and peaceful death with the help of our veterinarian. Euthanasia is accomplished by a lethal injection of drugs that literally puts the dog to sleep. Some veterinarians will administer this procedure in the client's home. Many owners wish to be present, holding their pet, when it is put to rest.

You will need to decide how you want to handle your pet's remains. Burial in the yard used to be a popular choice, but it is no longer feasible for many. Even if we have the space, it is often prohibited by local laws. Burial in a pet cemetery can be a good choice. Many choose to have their pet's remains cremated. The cremated remains can be returned to the owner for burial if so desired.

Allow yourself time to grieve your loss. Don't take to heart remarks made by those who tell you, "Get over it. It was just a dog." Your Airedale was much more than that. Losing a beloved companion takes time to accept. A dog is often the most nonjudgmental friend a person can have.

Children especially need to be guided through the grieving process and it can help if they understand that you, too, are grieving. Many humane societies, animal shelters, universities, and animal hospitals offer grief counseling. There are also good books available on the subject. You may find it helpful to write about your pet, a eulogy of sorts, that you can bring out some day to recall the good days you had with your Airedale. Consider making a donation in your pet's name to a local humane society, a veterinary health foundation, a pet-assisted therapy organization, Airedale Rescue, or any of the many worthy canine organizations that so badly need support.

You will never be able to replace your deceased pet, but the time will come when you realize that the house is awfully empty without an Airedale. When you choose your new pet, do not expect a duplicate of your old companion. Every dog is different, and these differences keep life interesting.

Feeding Your Airedale

Good nutrition is vital in maintaining the health of your Airedale. Airedales are not picky eaters—in fact, most Airedales will eat anything that doesn't eat them first! Proper feeding of high-quality foods can help your dog stay active and fit well into its teens. While it isn't necessary to be an expert in the field of nutrition to feed your dog properly, some basic knowledge will help you keep your dog healthy.

What should be fed, how often, and how much are all pretty subjective. Most people prefer a good commercial diet. There are commercial diets to fit any stage of life and just about any physical condition.

How Often to Feed Your Airedale

A healthy Airedale can do well on one meal a day, but many people prefer to split the daily ration into two meals. Active dogs especially can benefit from twice-daily feedings. With less food in the stomach at any time, the dog is less likely to suffer from gastrointestinal upset, particularly from bloat, which was described in the previous chapter, Health Care. Senior and convalescing dogs often benefit from several smaller meals a day rather than one large one.

Free-feeding

Some owners free-feed. This means that the dog always has food available and is free to eat when it wants. There are drawbacks to this system. It is difficult to assure the freshness of the food and to assess exactly how much the dog is eating. Many dogs will overeat and become obese if allowed to free-feed. Also, it is difficult to adapt this to a traveling schedule if you choose to take your dog on vacation with you. Free-feeding can also complicate housebreaking.

How Much to Feed

How much to feed your dog depends on many factors. Active dogs need more than sedentary couch potatoes do. Younger, growing dogs require more than senior citizens. If the dog is fed a "super premium" commercial food made with highly digestible, high-quality ingredients, it will need less than a dog fed a generic or house brand made from less digestible, lower-quality ingredients. Your Airedale should be fed just enough to maintain good weight. A dog in proper weight will not appear roly-poly. It won't have a roll of fat over the tail, a noticeable paunch, or "saddle-bags." A quick gauge of proper weight in a dog is that the ribs should be readily felt when you run your hands along its sides. There should only be a thin layer of muscle and very little fat in this area. On the other side of the coin, your Airedale is probably too thin if the ribs are visible or the points of its pelvic bone protrude. Dog food labels list recommended amounts to feed, but use this only as a rough guide; often, the amount suggested is too much for normal dogs.

How to Feed Your Airedale

Your Airedale should be fed in a quiet place. It should be given its meal and allowed approximately 15 minutes to finish. (Most Airedales seem to finish their meal before you even take your hand off the bowl!) If the dog hasn't finished in that amount of time, take the food away and don't feed again until the next regular mealtime. Exceptions can be made for sick, convalescing, or elderly dogs. If your dog turns its nose up at its meal, resist the temptation to add table scraps or other "people food" to make it more interesting. Constantly switching brands and types of food for healthy dogs should also be resisted, as this encourages finicky eating habits. You may find that your dog prefers one brand over another or maintains better condition with a certain brand, but once you have found a good food, stick to it. If you decide to change your dog's diet, do so gradually over a period of at least one week. Put just a small amount of the new food in with its normal ration at first, and gradually substitute more and more of the new food over time until the dog is eating the new food entirely. A sudden change can cause gastrointestinal distress. In spite of what your Airedale may try to tell you, it can't exist on a diet of pizza crusts, dead birds, steak, and sofa stuffing. Airedales are notorious for trying to make meals out of a large variety of unhealthy items!

Your Airedale's food dish should be washed after each use and water dishes should be kept clean. If a water bowl is also kept outdoors for your dog, make sure that algae is not allowed to grow in it.

Your Airedale should be kept fairly quiet for an hour or two after eating. Hard exercise and rigorous play right after eating can be very dangerous to a dog's health.

Basics of Good Nutrition

Dogs are carnivores, but they cannot thrive on meat alone. Actually, their dietary needs are more that of omnivores. This means that a dog needs a combination of foods—meats and other protein foods, grains and other vegetable foods to provide carbohydrates, fats to keep skin and coat healthy, fiber to maintain good intestinal health, vitamins and minerals to keep the complex workings of the canine body in balance. Water is also essential to the well-being of the dog.

Proteins

Proteins are required for growth, development, and repair of body tissues. They are necessary for the maintenance of hair, muscle, bone, and internal organs. Most dry foods formulated for normally active adults (adult maintenance diets) include a guaranteed minimum of 20 to 26 percent crude protein. This range differs in foods formulated for dogs with special needs, such as hard-working dogs, puppies, senior dogs, and dogs with compromised health. In commercial foods, proteins are supplied in many forms. Manufacturers may use the flesh of poultry, beef, lamb, pork, chicken, or turkey. Proteins can also be supplied in the form of meat by-products or poultry by-products, meals, or digests. While we may feel squeamish at the thought of eating a meal of lungs, spleens, stomachs, dried ground whole fish, or undeveloped eggs, they can be a nourishing source of protein for the dog. Vegetable protein is also used in commercial foods, and is commonly supplied by wheat, corn, rice, soy, barley, and other grains. The digestibility of certain protein foods is better than others, and the higher quality commercial foods usually include meat or poultry as one of the first three ingredients listed on the label.

Carbohydrates

Carbohydrate foods are used as a major ingredient to supply a ready source of energy for the dog's muscles and other bodily functions. They aid the brain and nervous system, and are needed to help digest other foods, especially fats. Common carbohydrate foods are corn, rice, barley, oats, wheat, kelp, whey, molasses, and sugar.

Fats

Fats supply concentrated energy and are vital for healthy skin and coat. Fats are necessary for normal growth. They also make food more palatable. Most dry foods formulated for normally active adult dogs contain a guaranteed minimum of 8 to 18 percent crude fat. Weight reduction and senior diets contain less. Puppy, performance and stress diets contain more. Common sources of fats are beef, lamb, and chicken fat, poultry fats, beef and other tallows, fish oil, corn oil, soybean oil, vegetable oil, sunflower oil, and flaxseed oil.

Fiber

Fiber is the part of food that is indigestible; however, this doesn't imply that fiber is worthless or not needed. Fiber provides the roughage or bulk necessary to help food residues pass through the intestines. Most dry foods formulated for adult dogs will contain a guaranteed maximum percentage of crude fiber from 3.5 to 6 percent. Weight control and senior diets generally contain a higher percentage

Vitamins and Minerals

Good commercial diets use a carefully formulated balance of vitamins and minerals. They include those that exist naturally in the ingredients used and that survive the cooking process, and supplements that are added to the basic ingredients. When feeding a good commercial diet, vitamin and mineral supplementation by the owner is rarely necessary, and should be done only under veterinary supervision.

Water

Water is an essential nutrient. It is vital to the proper functioning of every cell in the body. Without adequate water respiration, digestion, elimination, and metabolism will suffer. The amount of moisture included in commercial and homemade diets is not sufficient by itself to maintain good health. Clean, fresh drinking water should be available to the dog at all times.

Preservatives

All commercial dog foods contain some form of preservatives. Without preservatives, foods would spoil very quickly. Common chemical preservatives are BHA, BHT, ethoxyquin, and sodium nitrate. Tocopherols (vitamins C and E) are classified as natural preservatives. The use of BHA, BHT, and ethoxyquin has come into question and there is some debate as to the long-term health risks associated with their use. For those who are concerned about the use of these chemical preservatives, manufacturers of many of the high-end foods are now preserving their products with tocopherals. These foods have a shorter shelf life, especially once the bag has been opened. All pet foods, regardless of the type of preservative used, should be stored in a clean, dry location, away from excess heat and light.

Types of Food

Commercial diets run the range from very inexpensive generic foods to the more costly "super premium" foods. Some people decide on home cooking for their dogs.

Dry foods come in the form of pellets or crushed or broken biscuit. Both are commonly referred to as *kibble*. Dry foods can be fed straight out of the bag, or they can be moistened with warm water or broth to make them more appealing. They can also be mixed with a bit of good-quality canned food to make them more palatable.

Canned dog foods come in many varieties, ranging from expensive meat-based foods to lower-cost products that contain larger amounts of cereal grains. They are generally more palatable than plain dry food. If you feed a canned food diet exclusively, it is essential that you read and understand the label. You will notice that the "Guaranteed Analysis" section will be a bit different from what is listed on dry food. The primary reason for this difference is the larger amount of moisture in canned food. Canned foods may contain from 65 to 80 percent moisture, while dry foods contain only 3 to 10 percent. This affects the percentages of protein and fat shown on the label. Canned foods list a much smaller protein and fat content than dry foods. If canned foods are fed alone, without mixing with dry food, they must be labeled as complete and balanced. Some canned foods are intended to be used only as a supplement to other, usually dry, foods. Feed canned food just slightly warmed or at room temperature. Do not feed these foods cold. Any leftover food should be stored in the refrigerator.

Semimoist foods are usually formed and colored to please the human eye. These foods also contain a higher percentage of sugar, preservatives, and artificial colorings than dry foods. Most experienced dog folks recommend that if semimoist food is to be fed, it be limited to a very small percentage of the diet. The "Guaranteed Analysis" percentages of semimoist foods are lower than the percentages in dry food because of the higher moisture content.

Frozen foods. There are a few brands of frozen foods available to pet owners, but these are quite expensive and are usually only used to supplement a dry diet. As with canned foods, feed these slightly warmed or at room temperature, and refrigerate leftovers promptly.

Homemade food. Some owners choose a homemade diet for their dogs. The dog may be allergic to some of the ingredients found in commercial foods, or the owner may have his or her own philosophical or nutritional beliefs and does not think that commercial diets are appropriate. It is difficult to provide a balanced diet with home cooking, but it is possible. If you choose this method, check with your veterinarian before starting, particularly if you are feeding a dog that has food allergies. Your veterinarian may be able to supply you with recipes that meet your dog's nutritional needs. There are also books on the market with tested recipes for your dog.

Which Is Best?

Most professionals—breeders and other experienced dog folks—recommend feeding a high-quality dry food. As mentioned earlier, this can be mixed with a small amount of canned food and moistened with warm water or broth. A good rule of thumb is not to have more than 25 percent of the total mixture be canned food. An occasional addition of a bit of cottage cheese, yogurt, or cooked egg is always appreciated by the dog but avoid supplementing your Airedale's diet with table scraps.

How do you know which dry food is best? If possible, choose one of the "super premium" foods available through pet supply stores. They are not usually available at grocery stores. Meat, chicken, or poultry will be listed as one of the first three ingredients on the label. They are generally more digestible and the ingredients are usually of a higher quality than those used in other foods. Many of the brands found in the grocery store are also good, complete diets. In most cases, the main ingredients in these will be a grain, and not a meat or poultry product. If you choose to feed these, buy a product made by a reputable manufacturer. It is recommended that you avoid the generic or house brands as there is no certainty as to the quality, consistency, or completeness of the ingredients used.

Reading the Label

When you read the list of ingredients for a commercial dog food, the ingredients will be listed in descending order by weight. The first ingredient listed will comprise the majority of the weight. Some of the ingredients may serve more than one purpose. For example wheat, corn, rice, or barley may serve as a protein as well as a carbohydrate. A particular food type may be "split" when it is listed on the label. If a food lists chicken meal as its main ingredient, and then lists rice flour, ground rice, and rice bran as the next ingredients, rice products may actually make up the majority of the food by weight.

The Association of American Feed Control Officials (AAFCO) was formed to develop standards for animal foods. Reputable manufacturers follow their guidelines for nutritional content, testing, and labeling. Those who do will include wording in their labels to the effect that the food meets or exceeds AAFCO guidelines. If a food is intended for a particular stage of a dog's life (such as puppy formulas, foods for pregnancy or lactation, or adult maintenance diets) it will state this on the label. If the food is formulated for all stages, this will be stated.

Remember that food formed into cute shapes or bright, meaty colors is designed to please the purchaser's eye. The dog doesn't care what the food looks like; it only cares what it tastes like!

Supplementation

Some dog owners like to supplement their dog's diet with various vitamin and mineral products, oils, enzyme products, or other products intended to increase health, stamina, or appearance. If the food is a good, balanced product, little or no supplementation should be necessary. Oversupplementation is a bad practice. If you do decide to supplement your Airedale's diet, consult with your veterinarian and make sure you are using a quality product that is intended for use by dogs. Do not exceed the amount recommended.

Special Needs—Age, Illness, Weight Control, Stress

There are commercial dog foods available for just about any life stage or condition. Most people start their Airedale puppies on puppy food, which provides higher percentages of protein and fat and levels of certain vitamins and minerals that are needed by growing puppies. These puppy foods are usually discontinued between six months and one year of age, at which time the dog is put on an adult maintenance diet. Senior diets are also available. These are easily digested foods made of high-quality ingredients. The percentages of protein and fat will be less than found in other foods, and the amount of fiber will be increased. Many dogs

Foods to Avoid

Dogs should not be offered the following foods. Some may merely cause indigestion, but others can be very harmful or even fatal.

- bones from fish, pork, chicken, or other poultry
- chocolate
- corn cobs
- fried foods
- raw egg whites
- raw onions
- raw potatoes
- small beef bones
- spicy foods

Most people start their puppies on puppy food.

"Lite" diets. As with senior foods, they will usually be lower in protein and fat and higher in carbohydrate than maintenance or performance foods.

Special diets are also available for dogs with allergies to ingredients commonly found in dog foods. These will be recommended by your veterinarian if he or she feels they would be helpful.

Note: If your dog is on an allergy diet, remember that you must also check the ingredient listing on any biscuit or treat you give it.

Some Airedales have sensitive skin and are prone to skin and coat problems even though they may not have allergies. Many do better on a diet comprised primarily of chicken or lamb, rice, and barley.

"Performance" or "stress" diets are also available. These should be reserved for hard-working dogs such as hunters, sled dogs, police and other service dogs, and for some dogs on show, obedience, and agility circuits. They are also useful for dogs under significant levels of stress. Performance and stress diets are significantly higher in protein and fat than maintenance foods.

Treats

There is nothing wrong with giving your dog an occasional biscuit or treat. However, don't load down your Airedale with them; they should not become a significant percentage of the dog's diet. A biscuit at midday or bedtime is fine. The occasional carrot, apple, grape, bit of cheese, or lean meat is also appreciated, but table scraps are not recommended. Commercial treats like jerky and semimoist treats may be given in moderation.

can do well all through their adult life on an adult maintenance diet, but owners often choose to put their elderly animals on a senior diet.

Airedales with health problems such as kidney, heart, or gastrointestinal disease can be fed a diet formulated to maintain them in good health for as long as possible. These are available through veterinarians as prescription diets. Diets formulated for weight control are available through veterinarians, or can be found at pet food suppliers; they will often be labeled as

Training Your Airedale

Living with an untrained Airedale isn't for the meek, and quite a bit of training will be necessary to maintain your sanity. Airedales are extremely bright and learn quickly, but they don't perform just because you want them to. They have to know "why" as well as "what." Airedales are the original "Question Authority" dogs. They can be headstrong and independent and they tackle life with spontaneity and exuberance. The very traits that some might see as negatives are the things that attract us to the breed. Perhaps that is because we are quite like our dogs! You will need persistence, flexibility, and creativity, and you will *definitely* need to keep a sense of humor.

A Good Citizen

An unruly Airedale that has taken over alpha position in the family is a major pest. More seriously, an untrained, unsocialized Airedale can be a potential liability and possibly dangerous. Some Airedales—particularly males—can be quite aggressive toward other dogs. They must be taught that this behavior will not be tolerated. The Airedale is also a natural protector of home and family. While this trait is admirable, it must be channeled so the dog does not become overprotective. Good training pays off by teaching the dog good citizenship. Training also benefits both partners by strengthening the bond between the dog and its human companion.

Using Food in Training

Put a group of dog trainers together and you are likely to have lively discussions over the best way to train. One of the biggest controversies is the use of food in training. I strongly recommend using food when teaching very young puppies. I even recommend it as an *occasional* incentive or reward during advanced training. When properly used, and discontinued as soon as possible, food helps teach an Airedale to focus on the trainer instead of its surroundings. When improperly used, it results in a dog who works only when food is present.

Airedales tackle life with spontaneity and exuberance.

Positive Reinforcement

Another trend, "no force" training, employs the liberal use of food, clickers, or other motivators to teach a dog. This method relies on positive reinforcement solely, with very little or no negative reinforcement (physical corrections.) It is undeniably effective in early puppy training. Some swear by these methods for show training or to polish competition obedience training. I certainly agree a trainer should use as much positive and as little negative reinforcement as necessary, but it is naive to assume that a typical Airedale will never need physical corrections while training for real-life obedience. Airedales must learn what *not* to do as well as what we want them to do.

The one thing that just about every experienced trainer will agree on is no one method is foolproof for all dogs.

When Do I Start?

Training starts the day you first bring your Airedale home and continues throughout the lifetime of the dog. Starting with an eight-week-old puppy is ideal, but it is never too late—an Airedale is never too old to learn.

Home, Class, or Kennel Training—Which Is Best?

Home Training

Some owners opt for home training, hiring a professional who comes to the home and trains the dog or instructs the family in how to train the dog. An in-home trainer can help with more than just routine obedience exercises. He or she can help the owner overcome other problems such as fence fighting and door or gate charging.

Home training can also be tackled with the help of some of the excellent books or videotapes on training, but they do not cover every possible problem you may encounter. If the methods they demonstrate don't work with your dog, you will need to seek alternate solutions.

A home-trained Airedale must also learn to be obedient off its own turf, especially in the presence of other dogs. Its lessons must be reinforced away from home as part of the process.

Class Training

Enrolling in a group obedience class is an excellent and economical way to train an Airedale. In addition to teaching obedience, a good instructor can help you watch for and correct any problem behavior. Your Airedale will be exposed to all types of people and dogs. Most Airedales enjoy classes, and it isn't unusual for a dog to start whining in anticipation even before its owner has pulled into the parking lot.

Kennel Training

Other owners send their dogs to a kennel for training. The dog can learn obedience or any other specialized work the owner desires. If your Airedale is headed for a career as a show or hunting dog, and you don't have the time or desire to do the training yourself, kennel training can be a good way to achieve your goals. However, you must learn how to maintain the same level of training that was accomplished by the trainer.

Training Tools

The Leash

The leash should be 6 feet (1.8 m) long and ½ to ⅝ inch (12.7–15.8 mm) wide, preferably leather. A good leather leash is stronger, more flexible (after it is worn in) and easier on the hands than a nylon or cotton leash.

A long-line allows a trainer to get farther from the dog and still have physical control. Long-lines can be purchased or they can be made from a few dollars worth of supplies. A good long-line can be fashioned from strong, lightweight cord with a bolt snap tied on the end. These lines should be 15 to 30 feet (4.6–9 m) in length. Retractable leashes can also be used.

The Collar

The choice of training collar will depend on the age and personality of your Airedale. Young puppies should be trained in soft buckle or snap collars. Older puppies and most adult Airedales will do better in slip (choke) collars. These come in both chain link and nylon. If you choose chain, the best is a medium-size tight, flat link, such as a "curb link" collar. Nylon collars should have a diameter of ¼ to ⅜ inch (6–9.5 mm). Proper length is important. The collar should be just big enough to fit over the dog's head without forcing, leaving only 2 or 3 inches (51–76 mm) of slack when the collar is on. Too much slack lessens the collar's effectiveness. Prong or pinch collars are usually reserved for dogs that are too strong for their owners. They are also helpful with dogs that do not respond favorably to training in a slip or buckle collar for mental or physical reasons. When properly fitted and used, prong collars act like power steering. Dogs are very sensitive to corrections when wearing prong or pinch collars. *The convenience of prong collars should not be an excuse for not properly training a dog.*

Warning: Slip (choke) collars and pinch or prong collars should *never* be left on an unattended dog.

Electronic collars are useful for some very specific problems, but these should *only* be used under the guidance of a professional trainer experienced in the proper use of these training devices.

Before You Start

Make sure buckle or snap collars are snug enough that they won't slip off, but not so tight as to be uncom-

The proper way to put on a training collar.

fortable. Slip or choke collars must be put on correctly. When your dog is at your left, facing the same direction as you, the end of the collar attached to the leash (the active, or live, end) should run over the top of the neck toward you, through the inactive, or dead, ring. When the collar is put on correctly and a correction (a quick tug and release) is given, the collar will loosen as soon as the force is relaxed. If it is put on incorrectly, the collar will tighten, but it won't release. Prong or pinch collars should fit snugly. They must be opened to put on or take off. If you can slide one over the head without opening the collar, it is too loose to be effective.

Learn to make a proper correction. The typical correction is a quick tug on the collar, followed by a quick release. The collar doesn't remain tight. The strength of the tug should be no more than required to get the dog moving in the right direction or to stop an unwanted movement. A well-timed correction is administered the instant the error occurs. The quicker it is administered, the less force it requires and the more quickly the dog will understand what you want.

Learn to use your voice effectively. Commands should be clear, firm, and distinct and should project confidence,

Walk briskly and don't slouch when working with your Airedale.

Finally, it helps to know a little about the process itself. Dogs learn through repetition and consistency. First show the dog what action you want with a particular command. Repeat as often as necessary until it catches on. When the dog is getting proficient, gradually decrease the use of treats you may have used to help teach the behavior, but continue to praise. Treats at this point should be given to reinforce exceptionally good performances, if the trainer wishes. Finally, eliminate the use of treats altogether, but continue to praise. When the dog is working well in a relatively sterile setting, add distractions and train in different locations. Airedales learn quickly at first, and then the learning rate levels off, or even drops a bit after several weeks. This is frustrating, but normal. Airedales soon reach the end of this learning plateau and training will again progress nicely.

Basic Commands

The basic exercises are *sit, down, stand, stay, controlled walking, heeling,* and *coming when called.* All training methods presented assume that the dog is at your left side.

Sit

The easiest to teach is the *sit.* Here are three ways to accomplish this. The first is similar to that used in training young puppies (see page 18). Show your Airedale a bit of food with your right hand. Slowly raise your hand up and toward your dog's rear, keeping your hand fairly close to the dog's muzzle. As the dog follows the movement of your hand it will sink into a *sit.* Couple this with the command *"Jeep, sit."* As soon as he does, give him the treat and praise him. Repeat until he understands that *"Sit"* means "put your rump on the floor." As he becomes steady, give the food intermittently, and then discontinue it completely, but praise him every time he sits. Use the

not uncertainty. Airedales pick up on intonations very quickly. Commands should be loud enough for your dog to hear, but it isn't necessary to shout. Teach your Airedale to listen to you. High, squeaky tones should be avoided except when praising or encouraging an Airedale whose performance is flagging a bit. Use your dog's name before a command to get its attention.

A little basic knowledge of body language (yours and your dog's) will also help. Walk briskly and don't slouch. Project an aura of benevolent authority. Hesitant motions and slouched posture won't get this image across. Learn to read your dog's body language. If your Airedale is trotting along briskly, head and tail up, ears alert, eyes on you, the dog is telling you that it's enjoying itself and you have its full attention. If its tail drops and its ears droop, your Airedale may be confused or discouraged, or you may be overcorrecting it. If the dog shuffles along, watching anything but you, it's probably bored.

The sit is easy to teach.

hand motion as a signal for the *sit* command even after you have discontinued the treats.

For the second method, hold the leash in your right hand close to the snap, or put your right hand in the collar. Give the command *"Jeep, sit"* and pull up on the leash or collar, angling a bit back toward the dog's tail. Push downward on the dog's rump to get him into a sitting position. Praise him the instant he sits. You will be able to drop the push on the rump very quickly. Eventually, give the command without any physical prompting, and if he responds, praise him. If he doesn't, give a slight upward pull or tug on the leash.

The third method is easiest if you are kneeling on the floor next to your dog. Use the same upward pull on the leash or collar, using your right hand. With your left hand, apply light pressure just behind the stifle joints of his back legs (the equivalent of our knees.) This will tuck him into a *sit*. As soon as he understands what is expected, eliminate the tuck. This is a great method for stubborn Airedales.

Down

Teach the *down* next. The first method is similar to teaching a puppy. Have your dog sit. Show him the treat with your right hand, close to his muzzle, and slowly lower it to the floor between and a little in back of his front feet. At the same time, give the command *"Jeep, down."* As he lowers himself to get the treat, move your hand slowly away so that he has to lie down to get it. The instant he lies down, stop moving your hand, give him the treat, and praise him.

A variation on this involves the same motion of your right hand with the treat. Put your left hand in his collar or hold the leash close to the snap with your left hand. As you move the treat down with your right hand, apply a bit of pressure straight down on the collar. Release the pressure and give the treat the instant the dog is down.

If a more forceful method is required, hold the leash right by the snap with your right hand. Put your left hand on the dog's withers. Give the command *"Jeep, down"* and pull or tug the leash downward. At the same time, push gently down on the withers with your left hand. Or: Kneel next to your dog. Run the leash under your knees so you can have both hands free. Put your left arm over the dog's shoulders and lightly grasp his left front leg with your left hand and his right front leg with your right hand. Gently pull the front legs up and out, and lower him to the floor.

Warning: Don't do this too quickly; cracking your dog's elbows into the ground isn't conducive to the learning process!

Let me give a word of advice when choosing the command for this exercise. If you use the word *"Down,"* don't use the same word when you want the dog to get off the furniture or to stop jumping on you. Use the command *"Off"* instead so you do not needlessly confuse your Airedale. Or use a word other than *"Down"* to mean lie down. (One of my obedience students uses the command *"Crash."*)

Stand

Next, teach your Airedale to stand on command. (This is especially helpful for grooming or examining your dog.) Have your dog sit. Show him a bit of food with your right hand, close to his muzzle. Give the command *"Jeep, stand."* Slowly pull your hand away from him, parallel to the ground and on a level with his nose. As he gets up to follow the treat, give it to him as soon as he is standing. Stop his forward motion by placing your left arm just in front of his stifles. If he repeatedly jumps for the treat, don't use food. Instead, put your right hand in his collar to the side of his neck and pull gently forward to get him standing. Use your left hand to stop the forward movement as described in the first method. If you have a grooming table, you will find that this exercise is easy to teach on the table; he won't be able to move too far.

Sit-Stay

Now teach the *sit-stay*. Give the command to sit. Praise your dog and give the command *"Stay."* As you give this command, briefly show the dog the palm of either hand. (This will become the hand signal for *"Stay."*) Keep the collar loose with just a bit of slack on the leash. If your Airedale tries to get up or lie down, give a light tug upward and reposition it into the *sit*, repeating the command *"Stay."* Make this correction the instant the dog starts to move rather than waiting until it is standing or lying down. Don't allow your Airedale to get out of any *stay* until you have told the dog it may. This is the time to use a release word. Tell your dog, *"That's all!"* or *"Okay!"* and let it get up. Praise enthusiastically. Train your Airedale to allow you or a helper to pet it while it holds the *sit-stay*. (This is useful when teaching a dog not to jump on a person who greets it.)

Down-Stay

You'll teach the *down-stay* in a similar fashion. It may be helpful if you kneel on the ground next to your dog for the first few tries. Give your Airedale the command *"Down"* and the command and hand signal to *"stay."* Correct the dog back into position any time it attempts to get up, repeating *"Stay"* as you do. Try to get your correction in before the dog is fully up. For truly difficult dogs, you may find it helpful to step on the leash, fairly close to your dog. Allow enough slack on the leash and collar for the dog to breathe, of course, and to move its head normally. If the dog attempts to break, you will be able to correct it quickly. Give your release word and let the dog get up. If you started by kneeling next to your Airedale, work on having it hold the *stay* while you stand, eventually at the end of the leash.

The *sit-stay* and *down-stay* are taught by starting with the dog holding position for only a few seconds. When the dog is successful at that point, gradually increase the time it stays. Increase your distance, and then teach your dog to hold the *stay* while you move around. When your Airedale is steady on the 6-foot (1.8 m) leash, switch to the long-line. If you tackle this in small increments, it will not be long before your dog understands that it is to stay in position until you have released it from the command. Don't

attempt any off-leash stays until your Airedale is rock-steady on leash.

Stand-Stay

Next teach the *stand-stay*. Get your dog into the *stand* position, and give the command and hand signal to *stay*. Place your left hand just in front of the dog's stifles to prevent forward movement. If the dog attempts to walk forward or to sit, stop the movement with your left hand while repeating the *stay* command. As your dog catches on, stand up straight. Then, teach your Airedale to allow you to touch it while it holds the position.

Walking on Leash

Good leash manners are an absolute must. You should teach your Airedale two forms of walking on leash. Controlled walking is informal and the dog is allowed to do just about anything except pull or lunge. This is ideal for long walks. Heeling is more formal. The dog is taught to walk close to your left side, it adapts its pace to yours, and it sits automatically each time you stop—and the dog does all this on a loose leash. This is particularly useful when walking through a crowd or past a person who may be wary of your dog. It is also helpful when you have to pass other dogs on the street.

Start by teaching your Airedale to remain within 2 or 3 feet (61–91 cm) of you when you walk. Get a firm grasp on the leash, taking up a foot or so of slack in your hands. Begin walking, and as soon as your dog moves away more than this distance, let out the slack, turn and quickly walk in the opposite direction. (Be prepared: It only takes a second for the typical Airedale to lunge.) Don't give any warning when you turn and don't reprimand the dog. As it hurries to catch up with you, praise your dog and act as if nothing happened. Repeat until

Giving the hand signal to stay.

you are walking down the street. Hold the leash so that your dog will have to stay within 2 or 3 feet of you. Start your walk and watch your dog. At its first attempt to rush down the road, let out the slack and take a step backward before the dog hits the end of the leash. Use your *"Don't pull"* or *"Easy"* command. Call your dog back to you if necessary, patting your left leg to bring it back into the proper position. Praise your Airedale for returning and continue walking. Repeat if necessary.

It would be unreasonable to expect a normal Airedale never to forget its manners on leash. The instinct to chase will sometimes kick in before the dog can think better of it. Once your Airedale has learned the *"Don't pull"* lesson and is doing a decent job most of the time, you'll find that an occasional backward pop on the leash and collar will be just about all you need to keep your walks enjoyable. If some distraction has whipped your Airedale up into a real frenzy, stop walking and have it sit and stay for a few moments, focusing on you. When you have the dog's attention, continue walking.

your Airedale is no longer pulling, but is keeping an eye on you instead. If merely walking quickly away from the dog isn't sufficient, try running instead.

Warning: A running correction is not recommended for puppies less than six months or dogs with neck, back, or trachea problems.

Reinforce good leash manners by praising while your dog is walking on a loose leash, and be ready to repeat if it leaves the 2- to 3-foot circle around you. When your dog is doing well at this level, introduce distractions. Finally, add a command like *"Don't pull"* or *"Easy"* when you correct. This will become the verbal warning not to pull or lunge later on. This is the time to "take it to the streets."

Obviously you won't want to turn and run in the opposite direction while

Heel

Teaching your Airedale to heel will be easier if the dog first masters controlled walking. Start with your dog sitting at your left side, its head lined up with your left leg. Hold the leash in your right hand and gather up the slack so that the collar is loose and the snap hangs down, but the leash itself has very little slack. If the leash is interfering with your movement use your left hand to keep it up away from your legs. Give the command *"Jeep, heel"* and step off with your left foot, walking briskly. If your dog moves along with you without pulling, praise him. If he veers off to the left, turn right and continue moving. If he

60

lunges ahead, turn in the opposite direction and continue moving. If the dog bumps into you or tries to cross over in front, turn left into him. If he's interested in something behind him and he lags, surprise him by running forward a few steps. If he lags behind because he is unsure or worried, turn to face him and coax him to you. As soon as he catches up, continue in the original direction. Praise the dog each time he returns to heel position. You will eventually be able to correct minor movements out of position with light collar corrections. Plenty of praise, an occasional whisker tickle, or tiny treats offered while the dog is moving correctly help reinforce good behavior. Talk cheerfully to him when he is heeling nicely.

Heel and Halt

As soon as your dog is heeling along fairly nicely, start teaching him to sit each time you stop. Heel a short distance, come to a halt, tell your dog to sit, and tug lightly upward on the leash. Gently push on the dog's rump if necessary and guide it into a *sit* aiming the direction you are walking. Do several heel and halts giving the *sit* command at each halt. Then heel and halt without saying anything. If the dog sits automatically, praise him for being so clever. If your Airedale starts to sit and then hesitates, encourage him to finish. If he doesn't do anything, correct him into a *sit* with a light upward pop on the leash. Your Airedale will soon understand that each time you stop he should sit.

As you progress, introduce longer distances, turns to the right and to the left, and about-face turns. If your dog veers away from heel position on straight heeling, bring him back into position with collar corrections. Correct by tugging back toward you if your dog is too far ahead, up toward you if he lags too far behind, in toward

Help your dog understand the correct heel position.

Make coming when called an enjoyable experience.

you if he veers to the left. Don't allow your Airedale to move too far into the wrong direction before correcting; 6 inches to 1 foot (15–30 cm) out of position calls for a correction. Teach your dog to change pace with you and remain in *heel* position when you walk slowly, quickly, or run, using plenty of verbal encouragement. One way to help your dog understand the heel position when he is just beginning to learn is to hold a bit of food up next to your body in a manner that will make the dog automatically stay in the correct position. When your Airedale understands heel position, offer the treats only intermittently, and only when your dog has done a particular maneuver (such as a change of pace or a turn) in the correct manner. Finally, eliminate the use of treats altogether, but continue to praise.

Collar corrections are a quick tug or jerk and release action. Heeling corrections are given parallel to the ground, not in an upward direction. Don't keep the collar tight after a correction, and don't allow your dog to keep the collar tight itself by constantly pulling into it. Corrections should be scaled to the temperament and strength of your dog. Submissive dogs, dogs that have had bad experiences with prior training, and dogs that are very willing and attentive need very little in the line of physical correction. The right correction is the lightest one that gets the point across. Even with big, strong dogs a light, well-timed correction is usually more effective than a poorly timed major yank.

Your Airedale will become proficient pretty quickly at heeling in your backyard with no distractions. Expect it to forget everything when you first try to heel the dog past soccer practice or your neighbor's pack of wild Yorkies. Be prepared to back up to previous lessons when encountering new situations.

Come

Next to bad leash manners, not coming when called is probably the biggest complaint dog owners have. It isn't too difficult to teach your Airedale to come when it is called if you break the training down into small steps and don't try to skip ahead too fast.

A short lesson in dog psychology is necessary here. The quickest way to teach your dog to run in the opposite direction when you call is to call it to you for punishment or to do something unpleasant. If the dog's prompt response to your command results in something disagreeable, it will think twice before coming the next time you call. Instead of calling the dog for punishment or something distasteful, go to it.

The first step is to teach your Airedale to come running the instant she hears the command *"Possum, come."* Put her in a *sit-stay,* go to the end of your leash, and wait a few moments. Call her with the command *"Possum, come"* in a cheerful voice. Run backwards a few steps, giving a light tug on the leash if necessary. Praise her as she comes toward you. Repeat until she comes without your tugging on the leash. Now, call her to you while you are walking. As you issue the cheerful *"Possum, come,"* run backwards a few steps, retracing your original path of travel in reverse. Give a light tug on the leash when you start to back up so that she has to turn and run toward you. Praise and encourage her, taking up the slack as she gets close. Repeat until she understands the exercise. Now call your dog and give the *sit* command when she gets right up to you. Praise again. (The *sit* allows you enough time to take her by the collar or to snap on her leash, and it also helps her learn that she mustn't jump on you when she gets there.) When she is doing this well, snap on the long-line and let her wander around. Call her; if she comes from this greater distance, praise her. If she ignores you, give a light jerk on the long-line and run backwards just as you did on the 6 foot (1.8 m) leash. If she seems confused or hesitant when you call, squat down and spread out your arms to encourage her. Or run backwards or away from her to urge her to chase you. As she gets close, face her as she comes in the rest of the way. Most Airedales love the "chase me" exercise. Holding a small treat at about belt buckle height can help teach your Airedale to come in close and be centered on you. Discontinue the treats as soon as possible because it's vital that your Airedale learn to come *every* time you call, not just when you have food.

A good on-leash response is necessary before you can expect your Airedale to come when it is off-leash. When your dog is reliable on both the leash and on long-line, it's time to practice off-leash in an enclosed area. If your Airedale just plain refuses to come when off-leash, walk it down and snap the leash back on; the dog is not yet ready for prime time.

Remember that even a trained Airedale may not respond promptly to a recall if it's in hot pursuit of a squirrel or is intent on starting a scrap with another dog. Be realistic in your expectations. Some Airedales are never completely reliable off-leash.

Avoiding Training Problems

1. Airedales get bored quickly; short sessions twice a day may be better than one long one at the start. Even when you progress to the point where you and your dog are happy working for a longer time, put plenty of variety into your work. Don't repeat exercises needlessly. End each session with a good game. Break up difficult sessions with short play periods.

2. Watch for signs that your Airedale is confused. If your dog is having difficulty learning an exercise, present it in a different manner. Each new location and situation is a new experience. Never hesitate to back up to an earlier lesson your dog did well. Be creative.

3. Don't train when you are overly tired, angry, or rushed. Don't take out the day's frustrations on your Airedale.

4. Resolve to be successful and have fun. Many top performing Obedience Trial Airedales started out life as unruly, uncivilized house pets.

Aggression

What if your Airedale is dog-aggressive? A solid foundation in obedience is essential to maintain control. Stress eye contact and full attention on you during your training. Most experienced Airedale trainers will tell you that distracting your dog from an impending unpleasant scene is one of the most effective ways to deal with the problem. When you see your Airedale begin to hackle up, it's time to "change the subject." Quickly turn the dog away from the object of its attention and if possible, have it sit and stay, facing you. Get the dog's attention as quickly as possible, and when it is focused on you, heel it away to a neutral area. Aggressive dogs should never be allowed off-leash in any area where they may encounter other animals.

Grooming
the Airedale Terrier

Basic Coat and Skin Care

Expect to spend a significant amount of time grooming your Airedale during its lifetime. Even Airedales left in full coat need huge amounts of combing and brushing to look and feel good. An Airedale should be kept clean, but too-frequent bathing can dry out the skin. Regular combing and brushing is also essential in keeping your pet clean.

A grooming kit for the pet Airedale should include:

- a good metal comb
- a slicker brush (a brush with curved or bent wire bristles)
- a hard natural bristle brush
- a palm brush (a rubber-backed brush with blunt metal teeth that is worn on the hand)
- a wire-toothed terrier glove
- toenail clippers
- styptic powder
- blunt-tipped scissors
- liquid ear cleaner (available from your veterinarian or animal supply catalogs)
- cotton balls
- a toothbrush and canine toothpaste

A grooming table is a wise investment. This is a sturdy, collapsible table with a non-skid rubber surface. A post and noose can be attached to restrain a fidgety dog. A grooming table is an absolute lifesaver for your back as it brings your dog up to a convenient height.

Your Airedale's coat should be combed and brushed at least weekly, and more often if the dog has gotten into burrs, foxtails, or mud. Brush the dog out with the slicker brush if its coat is fairly long. If its coat is short, give the dog a good brushing with a natural bristle brush. The Airedale's furnishings, the longer hair on its legs and muzzle, can be worked with the palm brush to loosen dirt and break up tangles. Spray de-tanglers are also available, if necessary. The entire coat can then be combed out.

Flea and Tick Control

Flea and tick control is a must. Evidence of fleas can be found anywhere, but especially above the base of the tail, on the belly, and inside the thighs. If your dog has been in tick country, check for these pests as well. See Health Care for the Airedale Terrier, page 32, for more on this subject.

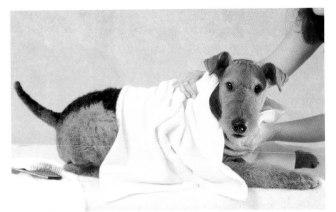

Your Airedale should be kept clean.

64

Caring for the Feet, Ears, Eyes, and Teeth

Toenails should be checked weekly and clipped at least monthly, although more frequent clippings are desirable. Guillotine clippers or the heavy scissor-type clippers are easy to use. Clip only the hook off the end of the nail, avoiding the quick. If you accidentally cut into the quick, the nail will bleed and it will be painful for the dog. Keep a container of styptic powder handy to stop bleeding in case of an accident. You may want to file the rough edges of freshly clipped nails. Check between the toes and pads for any hidden foreign matter. Clip or trim the hair between the pads so debris won't get trapped.

Clean the inside of your Airedale's ears, using ear-cleaning liquid and cotton balls. Clean the inside of the ear flap and as far as you can see down the ear canal. If the hair inside the ear has gotten long, pluck it out so debris won't be trapped. Carefully remove any debris, dirt, or hair that may affect the eye. Do not use any medication in your dog's eyes that has not been prescribed by your veterinarian.

Examine the area around your Airedale's eyes. Check for foxtails or other stickers that may get trapped.

Teeth should be brushed daily, using a toothpaste made for dogs. Teeth-cleaning products are available from your veterinarian, pet supply catalogs, and most pet supply stores. Your veterinarian may recommend a professional cleaning and scaling job, performed while the dog is anesthetized.

Grooming the Pet Airedale

Most owners take their Airedales to professional groomers for clipping and trimming, but some tackle the job themselves. Although the initial monetary outlay for clippers and blades can be considerable, money will be saved

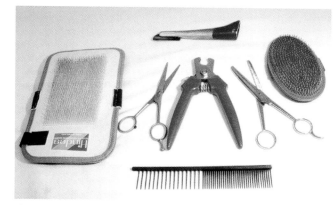

Grooming tools for your Airedale. Left to right: wire-toothed terrier glove, scissors, nail clippers, multi-toothed thinning shears, palm brush. Top: stripping comb. Bottom: metal-toothed comb.

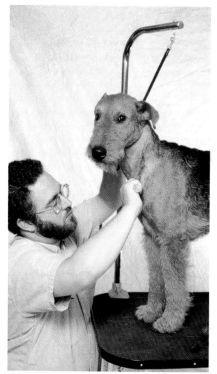

Stripping the coat will maintain good color and crisp, wiry texture.

65

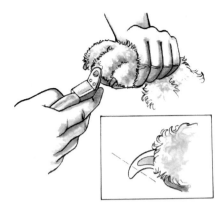

Your Airedale's toenails should be checked weekly and clipped at least monthly. Take care to clip off only the end of the nail. Cutting into the quick is painful and will cause bleeding.

in the long run if you groom your Airedale at home.

Clippers and Blades

The costliest piece of equipment you will need is a good clipper. You will also need several blades. The #5 blade is a coarse blade that is ideal for the body coat where the hair should be left longer. The #8½ or #7 blade are good choices for a medium blade. This is used on the head, rump, and underside of the dog. The #10 blade is a fine blade that cuts hair very short. It is used to trim hair between the pads on the feet, under the belly, and sometimes the ears. Good pet clippers are made by several manufacturers. You may also want to purchase a pair of multitoothed thinning shears.

Before You Clip

Your Airedale must be thoroughly brushed out, bathed, and dried before clipping. Dirty hair and mats will dull

blades prematurely, and can contribute to a painful condition called clipper burn.

You'll find it helpful to keep photographs of well-groomed Airedales handy while you are working, showing the side, rear, front, and a close-up of the head. This will provide you with outlines to refer to while you work.

Technique

Begin trimming with the coarse blade. Start at the top of your dog's neck and work down the spine to the tail. Clip down the ribs to the chest area, always working in the direction of hair growth. Be careful not to leave a "skirt" of hair on the chest. Now clip down the sides of the neck to the shoulders, and down the shoulder blade to the elbow. Clip the back of the haunches and the rump. Then clip the tail. Now, move to the front of the dog. Clip the throat area to the chest. When viewed from the side the finished front should present a "fish hook" type line from the underside of the jaw, under the throat, and down the legs. The chest hair should not puff out in front.

Now switch to a medium blade and clip the head. Start just above the eyes and work back down toward the neck. Clip from the outside corner of the eye backwards, and from the corner of the mouth backwards. Clip both the inside and outside of the ears.

Now clip the belly area, including the inside of the thighs. Clip carefully around the anus. Clip the belly area and the inside of the thighs with the fine blade. Some groomers also use a fine blade on the ears, especially if the Airedale has heavy or large ears.

As you clip, check the blades frequently. If they seem hot to the touch, take a break while they cool off or use an aerosol clipper cooling product to cool them more quickly.

Next, using scissors or thinning shears, blend the clippered areas into the unclipped hair so everything looks smooth. Carefully scissor-trim around the edges of the ears. Trim the eyebrows, but don't remove them entirely. Getting the proper trim on the head is the trickiest part of the job. Refer often to your picture of a well-groomed Airedale, and remember that it's much better to take off too little hair than too much! Comb out the beard and trim or thin the hair so that the head resembles a brick in shape.

Now you'll move to the legs. Brush out the furnishings and even them out by plucking the longer, uneven hairs or by scissoring carefully. The front legs should resemble tubes with straight sides. Trim the rear of the dog's back legs down to the hock, using the medium blade. Even out the rear leg furnishings as you did the front. Stand at the rear of your Airedale. Trim the hips and rear legs so that you have a straight line from the hip to the floor. Trim around the feet so they appear round and compact. A well-groomed Airedale doesn't look as if it's wearing bedroom slippers! Comb and brush it out once again and check for stray hairs.

Pet Stripping

Clipping an Airedale will result in the loss of some of the rich coloring and coarse texture of the coat. A compromise some pet owners choose is the pet strip, which results in most of the color and coarse texture remaining. Stripping is the process of plucking out long or dead hairs, either by finger and thumb or with the aid of a stripping comb. Stripped coat is pulled, not cut. You may cringe at the thought of pulling your pet's hair out by the roots, but wire hair is quite different from ours or that of non-wire-coated dogs. Long hair, especially when the coat is "blown" or fully grown out, is relatively easily removed. With pets this usually involves stripping out the black areas and possibly the shoulders, haunches, and skull. The throat, ears, cheeks, belly, and rump can be clipped. The following rough guide describes the process. Until you and your Airedale are used to stripping, you may need to spread this job out over several days.

Tools for Stripping

The tools you will need in addition to the ones already listed are a stripping comb and a rubber finger stall. You will find the hair easier to grasp if you wear a finger stall on your thumb. These are available at office supply or stationery stores.

Technique

Hold the stripping comb at a 45 degree angle to the skin and grasp a small amount of hair between it and your thumb. Pluck in the direction of coat growth. Only a small amount of hair should be removed at a time; if you pull too much at once it is very uncomfortable for your dog. Make sure you are not cutting the hair with the stripping comb. Grooming chalk in the coat can make the hair easier to grasp and hold. Remove at the minimum the longer hairs. Show groomers remove much of the hair, leaving the Airedale just about hairless in parts, but this isn't necessary in pet grooming. The body hair is left a bit longer than the hair on the shoulders, skull, and rump. Hair in these areas is stripped so that only the shortest hairs remain.

After you have stripped out as much coat as you want, clip the remaining areas. Use your multitoothed thinning shears to blend the sections together. Brush and comb out the legs, using the palm brush and comb. Pluck or trim the longer hairs to achieve the proper outline. Comb out the muzzle and pluck or cut the hair so that the head is brick-shaped. Scissor around the ear flaps and the feet.

There really was an Airedale under all that hair!

Even if you choose not to have your Airedale trimmed or stripped, you must keep the coat combed and brushed out. An untrimmed or unstripped Airedale's coat is very difficult to keep free of mats, dirt, and debris, and uncomfortable skin conditions can develop.

Grooming the Show Airedale

Show Airedales are never clipped, but are stripped instead. This is done in stages over a period of weeks or months depending upon the stage of coat growth when the job is started. I recommend you learn the art of preparing a coat for show from an experienced terrier groomer. Contact your regional Airedale club; many hold grooming classes where you will be guided step-by-step through the long process. If they don't offer classes, they may be able to refer you to a member who is willing to help you learn. The Airedale Terrier Club of America sells a helpful pamphlet, geared for the novice, called "How to Trim and Show the Airedale Terrier" and a more advanced book entitled "Grooming the Broken Haired Terrier," which will help guide you through the process. Videotapes on terrier grooming for show are also available but you will still find it almost imperative to work with an experienced person to complete the show grooming process successfully.

The Airedale Standard

Every breed recognized by the American Kennel Club has an Official Standard describing the ideal specimen. Think of the Standard as a blueprint for the physical qualities that make up the "perfect" dog. This perfection is what good breeders strive for, but the perfect dog simply doesn't exist. Many come close, however. If, like most of us, you find that your Airedale is a bit short of perfection, don't think any less of it. Most of us would never win Miss or Mr. America contests ourselves!

Official Standard for the Airedale Terrier

Reprinted with permission of the Airedale Terrier Club of America

Head—should be well balanced with little apparent difference between the length of skull and foreface. *Skull* should be long and flat, not too broad between the ears and narrowing very slightly to the eyes. Scalp should be free from wrinkles, stop hardly visible and cheeks level and free from fullness. *Ears* should be V-shaped with carriage rather to the side of the head, not pointing to the eyes, small but not out of proportion to the size of the dog. The topline of the folded ear should be above the level of the skull. *Foreface* should be deep, powerful, strong and muscular. Should be well filled up before the eyes. *Eyes* should be dark, small, not prominent, full of terrier expression, keenness and intelligence. *Lips* should be tight. *Nose* should be black and not too small. *Teeth* should be strong and white, free from discoloration or defect. Bite either level or vise-like. A slightly overlapping or scissors bite is permissible without preference.

Neck—Should be of moderate length and thickness gradually widening towards the shoulders. Skin tight, not loose.

Shoulders and Chest—Shoulders long and sloping well into the back. Shoulder blades flat. From the front, chest deep but not broad. The depth of the chest should be approximately on a level with the elbows.

Body—Back should be short, strong and level. Ribs well sprung. Loins muscular and of good width. There should be but little space between the last rib and the hip-joint.

Hindquarters—Should be strong and muscular with no droop.

Tail—The root of the tail should be set well up on the back. It should be carried gaily but not curled over the back. It should be of good strength and substance and of fair length.

Scale of Points	
Head	10
Neck, Shoulders and Chest	10
Body	10
Hindquarters and Tail	10
Legs and Feet	10
Coat	10
Color	5
Size	10
Movement	10
General Characteristics and Expression	15
Total	100

(Approved July 14, 1959.)

Points of the
Airedale Terrier

1. Muzzle
2. Stop
3. Skull
4. Crest
5. Withers
6. Shoulder
7. Back
8. Loin
9. Tail
10. Hip
11. Rump
12. Hock
13. Brisket
14. Elbow
15. Pastern
16. Chest

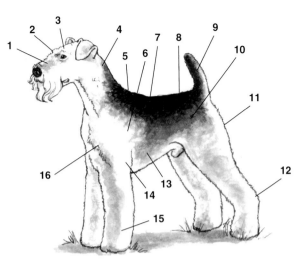

Legs—Forelegs should be perfectly straight, with plenty of muscle and bone. **Elbows** should be perpendicular to the body, working free of sides. **Thighs** should be long and powerful with muscular second thigh, stifles well bent, not turned either in or out, hocks well let down parallel with each other when viewed from behind. **Feet** should be small, round and compact with a good depth of pad, well cushioned; the toes moderately arched, not turned either in or out.

Coat—Should be hard, dense and wiry, lying straight and close, covering the dog well over the body and legs. Some of the hardest are crinkling or just slightly waved. At the base of the hard very stiff hair should be a shorter growth of softer hair termed the undercoat.

Color—The head and ears should be tan, the ears being of a darker shade than the rest. Dark markings on either side of the skull are permissible. The legs up to the thighs and elbows and the under-part of the body and chest are also tan and the tan frequently runs into the shoulder. The sides and upper parts of the body should be black or dark grizzle. A red mixture is often found in the black and is not to be considered objectionable. A small white blaze on the chest is a characteristic of certain strains of the breed.

Size—Dogs should measure approximately 23 inches (58 cm) in height at the shoulder, bitches slightly less. Both sexes should be sturdy, well muscled and boned.

Movement—Movement or action is the crucial test of conformation. Movement should be free. As seen from the front the forelegs should swing perpendicular from the body free from the sides, the feet the same distance apart as the elbows. As seen from the rear the hind legs should be parallel with each other, neither too close nor too far apart, but so placed as to give a strong well-balanced stance and movement. The toes should not be turned either in or out.

Faults

Yellow eyes, hound ears, white feet, soft coat, being much over or under the size limit, being undershot or overshot, having poor movement, are faults which should be severely penalized.

Versatile Airedales

The primary function of the Airedale Terrier today may be that of pet and companion, but Airedales are still proving their worth in the world of the working dog and maintaining the breed's reputation as a superior show dog. Airedales take the same intelligence, spunk, and humor to work with them that they display at home with their families.

Show Dog

The Airedale Terrier has always been a major player in the world of dog shows. Airedales are entered in most all-breed shows, but the cream of the crop will be seen at specialty shows, which are events that showcase a single breed. Winning a class, finishing a championship, or attaining one of the other top honors at specialty shows are highly sought-after goals for serious aficionados. The Airedale Terrier Club of America holds an annual specialty show for Airedales each October in Montgomery County, Pennsylvania, and "floating specialties" in other parts of the country. Airedale enthusiasts also show their dogs in specialties held by regional Airedale Terrier clubs.

An Airedale impeccably groomed and trained for the show ring is an impressive sight. Its general expression is one of haughtiness and superiority. It is a common practice in the show ring for judges to have a small group of terriers "spar" so that an assessment may be made of the dogs' terrier spirit. Sparring is the practice of bringing two or more terriers close enough that the dogs will take direct notice of each other, without actually making physical contact, resulting in each dog pulling itself together and showing off its self-confident, superior opinion of itself.

A dog must earn 15 points in competition by defeating other dogs of the same breed to finish a championship. Champions carry the initials "Ch" in front of their registered names.

How do you know if your Airedale has what it takes to be a show dog? First, make an assessment of its strongest points and shortcomings when compared to the Standard (see previous chapter). Then, seek the advice of a successful breeder, judge, or professional handler. Become involved in club activities, particularly grooming and handling classes. Many clubs put on matches, which are informal events where dogs and handlers can gain valuable experience in showmanship before entering American Kennel Club shows.

Obedience Trial Dog

Quite different from conformation shows, obedience trials are another field in which many Airedales excel. Dogs competing in obedience trials are there to be judged on the performance of certain prescribed exercises, not on appearances. Most obedience trial dogs are pets being shown by their owners. Unlike conformation, spayed and neutered dogs are welcome. Dogs with faults that would disqualify them from the show ring can be shown in obedience. Obedience Airedales can be shown in pet trim or no trim at all. A fair number of show dogs, including finished champions, also compete in obedience. It is truly

Many Airedales are excellent obedience trial competitors.

leash: *heel, stand for examination, recall* (come when called) a one minute *sit-stay* and a three minute *down-stay.* The second level, Open, requires the dog to perform all exercises off-leash. Dogs are tested on heeling, a drop on recall, retrieving on both the flat and over a high jump, and a broad jump. They are further tested on longer *stays,* with the handlers out of sight of the dogs. The next level, Utility, also requires the dog to perform all work off-leash. Dogs are tested on *signal exercises, scent discrimination, directed retrieving,* a *moving stand and examination,* and *directed jumping.* To earn the Utility Dog Excellent title, a dog must qualify in both Open and Utility at ten shows. To earn an obedience trial championship, a dog must earn 100 points competing in Open and Utility, by placing first or second in these classes.

Each year many Airedales compete in trials and earn titles. The best way to prepare your Airedale for this work is to participate in classes offered by a dog-training club. Many private trainers specializing in competition-level training also offer classes or individual training.

Tracking Dog

A world apart from dog shows and obedience trials are tracking tests, where specially trained dogs demonstrate their skills at following human scent trails. This sport is a natural for Airedales, and many compete each year. They have keen noses and the tenacity needed to tackle rough cover and difficult terrain.

There are four tracking titles offered by the American Kennel Club: Tracking Dog, Tracking Dog Excellent, Variable Surface Tracker, and Champion Tracker. Dogs earning the first three titles carry the initials TD, TDX, or VST after their registered names. Dogs earning *all* three are designated Champion Trackers, and the letters CT precede their names.

an exceptional Airedale that has earned both a championship and an obedience title.

Dogs earn titles by progressing through Novice, Open, and Utility classes. Judges employ standards describing the theoretically perfect performance of each exercise and dogs may not go below a specified minimum score to qualify. Qualifying scores are required from three different judges at each level. Dogs need not earn class placements to earn titles.

The titles, in order of difficulty, are Companion Dog, Companion Dog Excellent, Utility Dog, Utility Dog Excellent, and Obedience Trial Champion. Dogs earning the first four titles carry the initials CD, CDX, UD, or UDX after their registered names. Obedience Trial Champions carry the initials OTCH in front of their names.

At the first level, Novice, dogs are tested on their ability to heel on leash and to do the following exercises off-

At the basic level, Tracking Dog, the dog must follow a human track that has aged 30 minutes to two hours for approximately one-quarter (.4 km) mile. Except for two starting flags, the track is unmarked and the direction is unknown to the handler. The track contains several turns, and the dog must locate a small personal article dropped at the end by the tracklayer.

To earn the Tracking Dog Excellent title, the dog must follow a track that is much more complex, longer, older, and significantly more challenging than the Tracking Dog test. The track is crossed twice by fresher human crosstracks, and at least two obstacles such as roads, fences, creeks, or rockpiles test the dog's ability to handle physical challenges and changing scent conditions. Except for a flag at the start, the direction is unmarked and unknown to the handler. Four small personal articles left by the tracklayer must be found by the dog.

The newest AKC tracking title, "Variable Surface Tracker," is a more urban form of tracking, and the tests take place at sites such as industrial parks and school campuses. The dog must follow a track over vegetated, paved, and bare surfaces. A dog may have to work on exterior stairways, around buildings, across courtyards, through groups of bystanders or across parking lots, streets, and lawns. Like the TDX track, this track will be much longer, older, and more complex than the basic tracking test. VST dogs must find four small personal items on the track. This is a very challenging test.

Only highly skilled dog/handler teams pass the Tracking Dog Excellent and Variable Surface Tracking tests.

Hunting Airedales

Hunting is the original job of the Airedale Terrier, and there is a resurgence in the popularity of the Airedale

The premier showcase for the hunting Airedale is the Airedale Terrier Club of America's Hunting and Working Nationals in Ohio each year.

as a versatile hunting dog today. The premier showcase is the Airedale Terrier Club of America's Hunting and Working Nationals, held in Ohio each year. Here dogs are tested in retrieving, flushing, and fur tracking. Retrieving Airedales are tested on their abilities to retrieve ducks or other game birds from land and water, including single and multiple blind and marked retrieves. Flushing Airedales are tested on their ability to locate birds such as chukar or quail and to hold steady after flushing a bird. They must also mark the bird's fall after it is shot and retrieve it to hand. Fur tracking Airedales are tested on their abilities to track or trail the scent of a raccoon through varying terrain and cover. They must locate the tree in which the game is hiding and announce that they have found the quarry. These tracks are crossed by the scent trails of other animals and have dead-end false trails plotted along the way.

Junior, Senior, and Master Hunter titles recognized by the Airedale Terrier Club of America are currently awarded in retrieving, flushing, and fur at these events. A dog earning titles in all three fields at any level earns the coveted title of Junior, Senior, or Master Hunting Dog Versatile. A few regional clubs also offer tests during the year. Much credit is due to the Hunting and Working Committee of the ATCA in their efforts to promote the all-purpose Airedale and bring back the hunting and working skills that were in danger of being lost, at least in the show and pet lines.

Agility Trial Dog

This relatively new sport is the fastest-growing activity in the sport of dogs and is a natural for the Airedale. Agility dogs are tested on their abilities to maneuver their ways through a course of obstacles that include jumps, A-frame scaling walls, elevated "dog walks," swaying bridges, weave poles, seesaws, and tunnels. They are judged on a combination of speed and the ability to tackle each piece of equipment properly. Points are lost for refusals, knocking a jump down, or jumping off a particular piece of equipment too soon. The Airedale's natural speed and agility make this a sport in which our breed frequently competes and excels.

Search and Rescue

Search and Rescue organizations utilize highly trained, certified dog/handler teams to find lost people. They may work in wilderness searches or locate buried avalanche victims. They may be trained to locate bodies trapped underwater or search for victims in the rubble of collapsed buildings after earthquakes or bombings. There are several Search and Rescue organizations, and Airedales are participating along with the more traditional German Shepherd Dogs and retrievers. Once mature, well-trained, and taught to ignore "critters," skilled Search and Rescue Airedales are competent, valuable working dogs.

Airedales in Pet-Assisted Therapy

Pet-Assisted Therapy is the use of trained dogs to work with people in an institutional setting. These dogs are taken to nursing homes, hospitals, juvenile halls, schools for physically or mentally challenged children, and similar settings. They must be extremely friendly and absolutely reliable around people and other animals. These dogs have inspired seniors who haven't spoken in years to talk to them. They become trusted confidants of seriously troubled children. They provide a welcome break from the depressing daily life of long-term hospital patients. Many therapy dogs entertain patients or students with obedience demonstrations and tricks.

Quite a few Airedales participate in this valuable field. Pet-Assisted Therapy groups can be found by contacting your local humane society, Dog Training Club, or Kennel Club. Hospitals and nursing homes that take advantage of these services may also be able to put you in touch with local groups.

Breeding Airedale Terriers

Should My Airedale Be Bred?

Breeding is a controversial subject. It is painfully obvious that too many dogs are bred. Many deserving dogs are abandoned, passed from home to home, or surrendered to the local animal shelter where they may be euthanized because no homes could be found for them.

Primary Objectives

The primary objectives in breeding should be to improve the breed by breeding the best bitches to the best studs, and to produce puppies that are even better than their parents. Responsible breeders breed only from superior dogs: champions or show-quality dogs, or dogs that have proved themselves particularly talented in the fields of obedience, working, or hunting. A responsible breeder will not breed from a dog with health or temperament problems that may be inheritable. It is only through conscientious effort that the integrity of any breed can be maintained. People who breed dogs indiscriminately, without careful attention to health, temperament, and correct conformation, are responsible for perpetuating genetic disorders found in some breeds.

Possible Drawbacks

Most breeders do not make a cent from their activities. Special veterinary care, testing, and screening must be done before breeding. Even the soundest bitch can have trouble during pregnancy or whelping, requiring expensive veterinary care. The puppies will need tail docking and dew-claw removal, veterinary examinations, and vaccinations before leaving for new homes. Puppies can become ill or may be born with defects that will require surgical correction and neutering, or, if too serious, euthanasia. The increased amount of food the pregnant and nursing mother will need, as well as puppy food, add up. Stud fees are expensive, as are the costs of sending your bitch to the best stud if a suitable male is not nearby. Advertising the litter and registration fees must be added to the cost. The amount of money the puppies will bring in usually does not equal what was spent on the project.

Evaluate Your Motives for Breeding a Bitch

I urge you to evaluate honestly your motives for breeding. Your bitch may be the most wonderful pet in the world, but that isn't enough. If your main reason for breeding her is to get another just like her, this is chancy. You would do better by contacting her breeder and obtaining another puppy from the same lines.

How much do you know about the health background of both your own bitch and the potential sire of the litter? Are there any genetic problems in either line that may cause heartbreak to puppy buyers? Are you prepared for problems that may require expensive veterinary care and may even cost you the life of the puppies or their mother?

Will you be able to hand-feed the litter if the mother dies or is unable to feed the babies? Can you handle the chaos a litter of Airedales introduces into a household, particularly after they are on their feet, noisy and active? Will you be able to find suitable homes for possibly ten or more puppies? Are you prepared to keep puppies for as long as it takes to find suitable homes? Are you prepared to take back dogs if they do not work out in their homes? Will you be able to refund the purchase price of a puppy if something goes wrong unexpectedly?

Are you breeding to show your children "the miracle of birth?" This is not a great idea. The birth process is not necessarily a pretty one and things can go terribly wrong. Are you breeding because "a bitch needs to breed to be fulfilled?" This has never been proven true and spayed Airedales are excellent pets. Did you purchase your bitch as breeding stock or as a pet? Many breeders require that their pet-quality bitch puppies be spayed and not bred. If you made an agreement such as this with your breeder, you are obligated to honor it. Is your bitch registered? Is her registration a Limited Registration? Offspring of dogs with limited registrations cannot be registered. Most puppy buyers want registerable pups.

If you truly want to raise a litter of puppies and you can't accept *all* the responsibilities, consider volunteering to foster orphan puppies for your local animal shelter or humane society. You will be providing a valuable service for otherwise hopeless babies.

Warnings for Owners of Males

These caveats apply to owners of males, too. Most breeders will only breed their bitches to champions, or dogs with superior working abilities. Unless your male is one of these exceptional dogs and is in superb physical condition, free from genetic problems, do not use him for breeding. An Airedale used at stud may be more aggressive, especially toward other male dogs. He will also be aware of any bitch in season and try his hardest to get to her. Males do not need to go through the mating process to be happy. Neutered males are wonderful pets; they don't become fat and lazy unless you allow them to; ' and they are still good protectors.

As long as there are unwanted or abandoned Airedales in need of permanent, loving homes, serious consideration must be given before breeding *any* Airedale.

If, in spite of my efforts to dissuade you, you feel that you have a bitch worthy of being bred, the best advice I can give is to apprentice yourself to a good Airedale breeder with an established reputation. Consider asking your mentor if you can observe and assist in the process with one of his or her own bitches so that you will be better prepared if you breed your own dog.

The material presented in this chapter will not be sufficient by itself to provide all the information you will need as a breeder. It is only intended as a guide to the process. Your veterinarian will be a major source of information, as will the experienced Airedale breeders you should endeavor to befriend. Good books offering extensive advice on the subject of breeding are available and should be studied as well.

Preparations

Your bitch must be examined by a veterinarian before breeding to assess her general health and condition and to ensure that she is able to carry and whelp a litter. Her vaccinations must be up to date, as she will pass her immunity to the puppies. She must be tested for worms and wormed, if necessary, as these parasites can be passed on to the litter. She will be tested for canine brucellosis, and your veterinarian may recommend other tests as well. The owner of the stud dog will require that your bitch also have certain immunizations before you take or send her to be bred.

She should be X-rayed for hip dysplasia and the X rays should be evaluated by the Orthopedic Foundation for Animals (OFA) or by Penn-Hip. Only dogs free of hip dysplasia should be bred. Many Airedale breeders also have their dogs examined by a veterinary ophthalmologist to ensure that they are free of eye defects. Inherited eye diseases are being seen more frequently in Airedale Terriers than they have in the past.

No bitch should be bred on her first heat, or before she is physically mature. It is best to wait until at least the second or third heat period for breeding. Most professionals advise not breeding a bitch after seven years of age.

Finding the right stud isn't as easy as just using your friend's male Airedale, or even the closest champion male. Study and compare the pedigrees of both your bitch and the potential stud to determine compatibility. Most breeders linebreed, which is the practice of breeding dogs that are related, but at least one generation removed from each other, such as breeding a bitch to her grandsire or great-grandsire. *Linebreeding* is helpful in establishing a good, distinct line. *Inbreeding* should rarely be done. This is the practice of breeding mother to son, father to daughter, or sister to brother. *Outcrossing* is the mating of two unrelated individuals. Outcrossing is usually done to introduce new genes into a breeder's line, or to correct a fault the breeder has been unable to eliminate through linebreeding. The stud should be strong in the areas where your bitch is lacking.

A good place to start your quest for suggestions is the breeder of your dog. You can also check with other breeders for their opinions. Once you have made your choice, be sure you understand the terms of the contract you will be entering. Discuss the fee involved, and any provisions the stud's owner may have for a pick puppy from the litter. Determine what is to be done if the breeding does not take or does not result in live puppies.

The Mating

The female can be bred only during a short period of her heat cycle. Her first season may be as early as six months of age, but eleven to twelve months is still normal. These heat cycles or seasons usually occur about every six months, but longer periods are not unusual. Occasionally an owner won't notice the first heat. "Silent heats," which show few outward signs, are not unusual the first time.

The heat cycle consists of four phases. *Proestrus* is the first, in which the vulva will swell and there will be a bloody discharge. The bitch will be attractive to male dogs, but she will not permit a male to mount her. The second phase is *estrus*, in which ovulation occurs, and the discharge will change to a lighter, clearer color. The bitch will be receptive to the male at this time. The third phase is *diestrus*, which occurs when the female will no longer breed. She will not accept a male, discharges cease, and her vulva returns to its normal state. *Anestrus* is the last phase, when the system "rests" until the cycle begins again.

The bitch is bred during the estrus phase of her season, and the mating is usually done at least twice. A veterinarian can perform blood tests or vaginal smears to help narrow down the most likely time for a successful breeding.

Most bitches turn into real hussies during heat, and they may not be particular as to whom they will accept. Keep her protected because she will send her signal to every intact male within a mile radius of your home. Don't assume that a fenced yard is safeguard enough to protect your bitch from accidental breeding. Determined males can climb or dig their way to her in a surprisingly short amount of time.

It is recommended that you have an assistant during the mating process. Introduce the dogs in a small enclosed area. It may be advisable to keep both on leash at first. The bitch may be held if necessary to prevent her snapping at the male when he attempts to get down to business. The male will mount the bitch, and if the mating is successful, the "tie" occurs. A portion of the male's penis will swell and prevent it from being withdrawn for a period of time, sometimes as long as a half-hour. The male will turn around, but they will remain "tied" together until the swelling subsides. Don't attempt to separate the dogs during the tie; you can cause injury by doing so.

Whelping box with guard rail to protect puppies.

Pregnancy

Pregnancy can be confirmed by X ray or ultrasound. A veterinarian or experienced breeder may also be able to palpate the puppies during a short period of time about three weeks into the pregnancy. Pregnancy lasts around 63 days.

A bitch will start needing increased amounts of food about halfway through her pregnancy. She should be fed twice a day with food formulated for pregnant bitches. Some breeders feed the bitch a good puppy food during this period. During the last half of her pregnancy she will need about 50 percent more food than she normally eats.

Exercise is beneficial, providing it isn't excessive. Avoid the most strenuous workouts, such as running, climbing, and jumping.

Follow your veterinarian's advice on examinations during your bitch's pregnancy. Keep his or her phone number handy, as well as the number of the local emergency veterinarian.

Whelping Supplies

Now is the time to start preparations for the whelping area and nursery. This should be a warm area away from the flow of household traffic. This is also the time to start collecting the rest of your supplies.

1. You will need a whelping box for the mother and newborns. This should be easily cleanable and should have sides high enough to keep the puppies inside. A safety rail should be built into the sides to minimize the chances that the dam might accidentally smother a puppy when she lies against the side of the box. An exercise pen or similar fencing to keep the puppies contained will be needed as soon as they are able to climb out of the box. Introduce your Airedale to the whelping box about two weeks before the puppies are due. Cover the floor of the box with a thick layer of papers and keep a supply on hand. A travel crate, with the door removed, will be a useful piece of nursery furniture. The puppies will become accustomed to a crate from the very start, simplifying future crate-training.

2. Stockpile a good supply of washable bedding.

3. A large supply of paper towels, puppy-safe disinfectant cleaner, cotton balls, plastic trash bags, and cloth towels should be on hand.

4. A rectal thermometer, alcohol, heating pad, blunt-tipped scissors, and hemostatic forceps will all be needed.

5. Obtain a baby scale, a notebook in which to record weights and other notes, and rickrack or ribbon in assorted colors for identification collars.

6. Purchase a comprehensive book on breeding and whelping and read it *before* whelping; you won't want to have to read it in a panic while the puppies are being born!

Whelping

About a week before the puppies are due, trim the hair from your bitch's nipple area. Her temperature will drop about 12 to 24 hours before delivering the puppies, so start taking her temperature a couple of times a day a few days before you think they are due. You will know you are getting close when she loses her appetite and exhibits nesting behavior. She may shred her bedding or newspapers and she may start carrying favorite objects around.

When whelping is imminent, your bitch will become restless. Digging and tearing her bedding becomes intense. She may pant and shiver. She should now be confined to the nursery. If she needs to eliminate, she should be taken out on leash and then returned. If left unsupervised, she may choose to give birth under the deck or porch, in a closet, or some other inconvenient and possibly unsanitary location.

Each puppy usually arrives in its own package, the amniotic sac. Ideally, the mother will tear this open, lick the puppy, and bite through the umbilical cord. Be prepared to perform part of this function if the bitch doesn't; they are often unsure of what to do with the first pup. Tear open the sac if necessary, starting at the head. If the bitch doesn't take over at this time, remove the sac and stimulate the newborn's breathing by rubbing it with a clean towel. Make sure its nostrils are free of fluid.

If the bitch does not tear the umbilical cord, cut it yourself. Clamp it with the forceps, about an inch from the pup, and cut it between the forceps and the placenta. Dab the end of the cord with alcohol or iodine and tie a bit of dental floss around the end. The expulsion of the placenta usually follows the birth of each puppy. Many bitches will want to eat the placenta, and this is natural. The puppies should be placed next to the mother immediately for nursing. Allow her to relax between births, which may be

The mother with her new family.

79

from 15 minutes to an hour or more apart. The entire process may take as long as 12 hours, and sometimes up to 24 hours.

If There Are Problems

If the bitch has strong contractions every few minutes for 30 minutes without producing a puppy, contact your veterinarian immediately. Delay at this point could possibly prove fatal for the puppies or even the mother. Some of the things that can go wrong at this point are difficulty whelping a very large puppy or one in an abnormal position, or uterine inertia. A cesarean section may be called for.

After Whelping

Weigh each puppy and record its weight in your notebook. Tie a bit of different colored ribbon or rickrack around each puppy's neck (not too tightly!) so that you can keep track of each individual's progress.

Remove whatever soiled papers you can after each birth and replace them with fresh. When the litter has been born you can clean the whelping box and supply it with fresh bedding. When you have to remove puppies for cleaning or weighing, keep them warm. Transfer them into a warm, towel-lined box if necessary for a short while. Gently bathe the bitch's rear and dry it thoroughly. She may be reluctant to leave her new family, so you may have to lead her outdoors to relieve herself. Offer her water and a small amount of food, but don't be surprised if she chooses not to eat for a while. And don't be surprised if she vomits some of the placentas she has eaten.

The bitch may show a brownish or reddish vaginal discharge for several weeks after delivery, but if you notice pus, blood, clots, or a foul odor contact your veterinarian immediately. If she goes off her feed, this may be a sign of infection. Check her nipples daily to be sure all are producing milk. A bloody discharge from a nipple is a trouble sign calling for veterinary attention.

Danger Signs

There are several other problems to watch for at this time. Sudden neglect of the litter is a danger sign. A tender abdomen and elevated temperature may indicate a retained placenta. Uterine infections need immediate care. Infections in the mammary glands can cause rejection of the puppies, or she may be unable to produce milk at all.

Eclampsia is a life-threatening condition caused by a depletion of calcium. Symptoms include restlessness, irritability, disorientation, fever, twitching, and an increased heart rate. Convulsions occur in advanced stages. Immediate veterinary care is required if the bitch is to survive. Contact your veterinarian promptly about *any* condition that does not seem right.

The Newborn Puppies

The puppies should begin to nurse immediately after birth. The first feedings contain colostrum, which has the natural antibodies and immunity that are passed from the mother to the newborns. Keep an eye on the new family, and make sure all are being fed. If the mother rejects a puppy, it should be examined by the veterinarian. If the puppy survives, you may have to hand-feed it. If the litter is very large, the mother may not be able to feed them all adequately and you may have to hand-feed.

Newborn Airedale puppies average 10 to 12 ounces (285–345 g) at birth, and a healthy puppy should approximately double its birth weight in the first ten days. A newborn may lose a few ounces in the first two or three days, but if it does not start regaining weight within three days, the puppy may be in trouble. Monitor the weight of each puppy every day to be sure that each is eating properly and growing as it should.

For the first week or so the puppies cannot urinate or defecate by themselves. The mother will lick the puppies' abdomens to stimulate elimination.

Baby Airedales do little besides eat and sleep for the first week or so. They cannot see or hear at this time, but their sense of smell and instinct to stay warm are well developed. At about 14 to 15 days of age their eyes will open. Puppies will begin to get on their feet at about the same time their eyes open, and they will become increasingly active as they get older.

Dewclaws should be removed when the puppies are three or four days old. This is done for the future health and comfort of the pups, as dewclaws can snag and tear easily. This is also the time to dock the puppies' tails. Many breeders remove the dewclaws and dock the tails themselves, or they seek the assistance of an experienced Airedale breeder to handle this chore. If the tails are docked by your veterinarian, make sure he or she understands just how much of the tail is to be removed. Approximately two-thirds of the tail is left remaining. Tail length is an important part of the physical profile of the Airedale; too short a tail can ruin the outline.

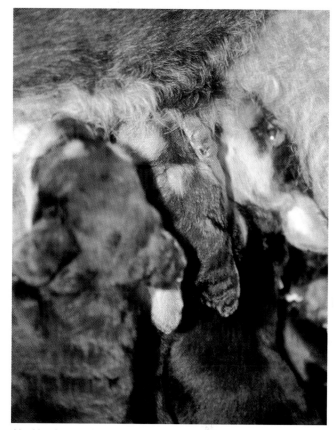
Healthy, hungry Airedale puppies, one month old.

Early Puppy Care

Weaning

Weaning starts when the puppies are about three and a half weeks old. Many breeders follow these steps: Make a gruel of puppy kibble, ground to a coarse meal, and commercial milk replacement formula. Place this in a shallow pan. Bolder pups may investigate on their own, but others may need to be coaxed. Place a small dab on the puppy's tongue or the tip of its nose to pique its interest. For the first week, the puppies will be wearing more food than they eat and their mother will still be providing most of their nourishment. During the following week soak ground puppy kibble (or whole kibble if it is small) in warm water for 20 minutes to a half-hour. After soaking, add milk replacement formula. The mother will not be spending all her time with the puppies at this age. She may visit several times a day for nursing after the puppies have been offered their prepared food. When the puppies are five weeks of age, you can add a bit of canned puppy food to the mix and the milk replacement formula can be discontinued. At this period the mother should be nursing the puppies only a couple of times a day, after feeding. As the puppies catch on to the process they will demand less milk from the mother, and her supply will begin to dry up. Begin to decrease the size of her meals at this time. The mother should be separated from the puppies by seven weeks of age so they will be accustomed to eating puppy food by that age.

Puppies develop rapidly—in what seems like no time at all they will turn into active youngsters. Their path to young adulthood is separated into several distinct stages. One important stage lasts from 21 through 28 days of age. Pups experience a rather abrupt development of the senses during this week and greatly need their mother and a steady, dependable environment. During this stage take care not to frighten or stress the puppies; this can cause lasting psychological damage.

Socialization

Good breeders introduce their puppies to a variety of things during the socialization period, which is the next stage. This lasts from 28 to 49 days and, to put it simply, this is when Airedale puppies learn to be dogs. As they play they will be learning about body language, vocalization, biting. They will learn just how much they can get away with before Mom reacts, and they learn to accept discipline from her. Puppies should not be placed in new homes during this stage. They need this time with their mother and littermates to learn.

New surfaces, playthings, sounds, and humans (including careful introduction to supervised and considerate children) should be introduced to the litter. The puppies should be conditioned to accept friendly eye contact with humans at this time and they should be handled frequently.

The human socialization period lasts from seven through twelve weeks of age, and this is the optimum time to place a puppy in its new home. The pup will rapidly bond to its new family during this period. The pup should be introduced carefully to new experiences: odd noises, traffic, strange people, other animals, and other situations that will help prepare it for the future. During this phase another important period occurs. From the age of eight weeks to eleven weeks the puppy will be in one of the critical fear periods. Traumatic experiences during this stage will have a lifelong effect.

Orphan Puppies

Sometimes, in spite of the best of care, something will go dreadfully wrong and the mother will not survive an infection, eclampsia, or some other condition brought on by pregnancy or whelping. In this sad event, raising the puppies will be solely up to you. Keeping the puppies warm is critical. An incubator is ideal, but a heat lamp over the whelping box may suffice. When using a heat lamp, cover a portion of the whelping box so the puppies can get away from the constant light. Hot water bottles and heating pads may burn a very young puppy, so a more remote source of heat is preferable. The temperature should remain at about 90°F (32°C) for the first week, after which it can slowly be decreased to 85°F (29°C). When the puppies are three weeks old, the temperature can be reduced again to 75°F (23.9°C), and in another ten days it can be reduced to about 70°F (21°C).

Orphan puppies must be hand-fed. Milk replacement formula is available through veterinarians and many pet shops. The puppies must be fed six to eight times a day until they are three weeks old, and then four times a day until they are six weeks old. Tube-feeding is a safe and easy-to-learn method for feeding orphan puppies, and it can also save time when there are many to feed. A soft, flexible tube is passed through the mouth into the stomach and food is given by syringe through this tube. Tube-feeding also lessens the chance of pneumonia brought on by aspirating formula. Hand-fed puppies must be "burped" just like human infants. Your veterinarian can instruct you on the proper use of stomach tubes. Puppy nursing bottles are also available for feeding. Eyedroppers are not recommended.

Orphan puppies will need help urinating and defecating for the first week or so of life. Moisten a cotton ball or cloth with water or baby oil and gently rub the anus and genital area to encourage elimination. This must be done after each feeding.

Orphan puppies will not have the social and developmental benefits of being raised by their mother, and may develop differently from other pups. Socialization is all the more important in the case of an orphaned litter.

Care of the Mother

Your veterinarian should examine the new mother a day or two after delivery to ensure that all is well. For the first week she will be engaged full-time in mothering her new family. Don't be surprised at a personality change at this time; many bitches become extremely protective of a new family. She may be reluctant to leave the litter long enough to eat and eliminate, so you may need to coax her out of the whelping box. If she is picky about eating, offer her healthy treats like cottage cheese, broth, liver, or chicken to entice her to eat.

Examine her nipples daily to see if the puppies have been scratching her. If the babies have been causing discomfort with their nails, clip them back. Be careful not to cut into the quick; cut just the tips.

An increased amount of a diet formulated for lactating bitches will be required to keep the new mother in good condition. A nursing bitch needs up to three times her normal amount of food during this period. High-protein foods such as cottage cheese, eggs, and liver may be added. Ask your veterinarian about feeding a vitamin-mineral supplement at this time.

Registering the Litter

Apply to the American Kennel Club to register the litter as soon as the puppies are born. Litter registration is required before the new owners can register the puppies individually. When the application form has been processed by the AKC, they will send you a packet of blue registration application forms for the puppies. You will complete the individual applications as each puppy is sold.

Matching the Right Puppy to the Right Home

Matching puppies to buyers is a big responsibility. You have observed the litter over the past seven or more weeks, and you will have become familiar with the pups' individual personalities. It is helpful to make notes as they grow, with observations as to their individual traits. If you are using different colored ribbons as identifying collars, it is easy to record accurate information for each puppy.

Some breeders perform puppy aptitude testing at seven weeks. These tests provide a basic personality profile for each puppy, giving the breeder and potential buyer a good idea of the

It's important for Mom to want a puppy.

the Airedale? Make sure their mental picture of the Airedale is realistic.

5. Do they own any dogs now? You may not want to place a male puppy in a home with a male dog already in residence. If the previous dogs are no longer with the family, what happened to them?

6. Have they already picked a veterinarian?

7. Do they have a fenced-in yard? If not, how do they plan to exercise the dog?

8. Do they work all day? What arrangements will be made for the puppy while they are gone?

9. Are they willing and able to train the dog and are they aware that considerable early socialization is necessary?

10. How do they react to your adult Airedale? If they are uncomfortable around or indifferent to her, how will they treat the puppy when it grows up?

Answers to these questions will assist in determining who will be a responsible dog owner.

The Puppy Kit

Send a puppy kit home with the new owners containing the registration application and pedigree, a supply of food, and the puppy's health records. Buyers will also appreciate a photograph of the mother and her babies. Consider including a suitable toy or two. Be ready and willing to talk to your puppy buyers as often as necessary. Consider having the buyer sign an agreement that he or she will return the dog to you if the buyer can no longer keep it. Responsible breeders do this; it helps keep Airedales from landing in the local animal shelter or from being passed from home to home.

Ear-setting

At about four months of age, when the puppies begin teething, you will

temperament and aptitude of each individual. These tests can be particularly valuable in selecting puppies who may become working dogs. One source of excellent, detailed information on testing and interpreting the results is presented in *The Art of Raising A Puppy* by The Monks of New Skete. Boston and Toronto: Little, Brown, 1991.

Interview the Prospective Buyer

Do a thorough interview of each prospective puppy buyer. A fat wallet and the desire to own an Airedale are not enough to qualify a person as an ideal owner. Find out the following:

1. Do they have children and if so, how old are they?

2. Find out if Mom really wants a puppy. In spite of a child's promises, she is going to be the one who will be taking care of the dog.

3. Have the prospective buyers ever owned a dog before?

4. Have they ever owned an Airedale? If not, why did they choose

Adolescence can be a trying time.

need to be able to help your puppy buyers with any necessary ear-setting. Airedale puppies' ears have a tendency to droop during this period, and by temporarily setting the ears in place with a dab of surgical glue there is a better chance of having good permanent ear carriage. Proper ear carriage is an essential characteristic of proper Airedale expression. Make sure you know the technique or can refer your puppy buyers to a breeder who will be able to help them at this time.

Responsible Dog Ownership

Being a Good Neighbor

Be considerate of your neighbors and keep their comfort and sanity in mind. Most dog-related complaints to the authorities come from disgruntled neighbors. When choosing the location for your dog's run or potty area, the best spot may not be just outside your neighbor's kitchen or bedroom windows. Scoop up feces from the yard at least daily and deposit them in a container with a tight-fitting lid. Use a deodorizer such as Odor Mute or Nilodor Deodorizing Cleaner periodically to wash down the run if a urine odor builds up.

When you walk your dog, carry plastic bags for cleanup. Considerate dog owners will not leave their dog's feces on the sidewalk or in the neighbor's yard. Scooping poop is not a job anybody enjoys, but ignoring a pile your dog has just left won't endear you to anybody. Keep your dog leashed unless you are in a public dog park or your yard. Don't let your Airedale roam the neighborhood. A dog that runs free quickly becomes the neighborhood nuisance. Loose dogs also often band together into packs, terrorizing other pets, livestock, wildlife, or even humans. An Airedale on the loose is apt to become a fighter, a car chaser, or, worse yet, a statistic. Too many dogs die on the streets in accidents.

Dog Laws

Most communities have laws regulating dogs. Most require rabies vaccinations and licenses. Leash laws abound, and these are as much for the safety of our dogs as for the peace of the neighborhood.

Many folks are frightened of or just plain dislike dogs. Great as you think your Airedale is, it won't be welcome in their yards or following them down the street. In the few areas where leashes are not required, dogs must still be under solid voice control. "Pooper scooper" laws are a reality in many cities.

Noise ordinances may govern the amount of barking your dog can get away with without being declared a public nuisance. Train your dog not to be a nuisance barker in order to avoid costly fines or citations.

Restrictions may also be placed on the number of pets that can live at any one address. If you already own a dog, check with your local jurisdiction as to these limits.

"Dangerous Dog" laws have been enacted in many cities. They severely penalize the owners of dogs that bite people, other pets, or livestock. It is your obligation to properly train and socialize your Airedale and keep it under control so that it does not frighten or attack a person or another animal.

Restrictive Dog Legislation

Restrictive dog legislation can extend far beyond licensing, leash laws, pooper-scooper ordinances and laws against dogs that have attacked people or livestock. Dog owners and breeders face a variety of zoning issues, including property setbacks of dog facilities and restriction of dog-related businesses. Breeding restrictions or outright bans also have been proposed in many areas.

Strict limitations of the ownership of certain breeds, particularly the fighting and guarding breeds, have been proposed by cities, counties, and states. Breed-specific "Dangerous Dog" legislation could ultimately result in the near extinction of many fine breeds, including the American Staffordshire Terrier, Staffordshire Bull Terrier, Bull Terrier, Rottweiler, Mastiff, Bullmastiff, Akita, Doberman Pinscher, and others. If dog owners permit this roster to grow, other protective, energetic, strong dogs—the Airedale, for example—could be added to it in future legislative campaigns by anti-dog activists.

Be aware of proposed dog legislation in your own city, county, and state. Through local and regional clubs, you can help defeat or modify proposed overly restrictive dog legislation, and assure that your rights as a responsible Airedale owner are protected.

Well-behaved Dogs

Many feel that there are too many restrictions placed on their lives already, without adding dog laws to them. However, everybody in the community, even the one who dislikes dogs, has the right not to be annoyed by our pets. *Responsible* dog owners and well-behaved, properly trained dogs do a great deal to help prevent even more restrictive legislation in the future, especially as our towns and cities become more crowded.

And never forget your main responsibility. Love your Airedale.

Finding Out More About the Airedale

The Airedale Terrier Club of America (ATCA)

The ATCA promotes and supports the participation of Airedale Terriers in many arenas: Conformation, Obedience, Hunting, Tracking, Agility, and other working fields. The national Specialty Show and Obedience Trial is put on by the club each year in Montgomery County, Pennsylvania, as well as at least one "floating" specialty in another part of the United States yearly. The club also sponsors rescue activities to help care for and place Airedales that are down on their luck.

The ATCA provides information and expertise in the fields of canine-related legislation, judges' education, public education, health matters, and just about any other Airedale-related field. They publish an excellent magazine that provides informative and entertaining articles.

The club provides two pamphlets free of charge to people interested in finding an Airedale: the "Puppy Buyer's Guide" and "Breeder Referral." Several other Airedale publications are available for sale.

Regional Airedale Terrier Clubs

At present there are 21 regional Airedale Terrier Clubs. These smaller organizations promote the breed in all its endeavors on a more local scale in much the way that the Airedale Terrier Club of America does on a national scale. In addition to offering Specialty shows and sometimes Obedience Trials and Hunting Tests, regional clubs often offer matches, grooming classes, obedience classes, educational events, newsletters, and social activities for their members. Local rescue efforts are also sponsored by these clubs. Serious Airedale fans should consider membership.

What could be better than owning one Airedale? How about several?

In Summary

The Airedale Terrier may be one of the "new kids on the block" compared to ancient breeds such as many of the hounds, but it has established quite a reputation for itself in the slightly more than a century it has been in existence.

Airedales are masters of the unexpected. They are intelligent and inquisitive, but they can be stubborn sons-of-guns. They are affectionate and loyal, but often display a definite independent streak. They can be the star performers in Obedience Trial competitions one day, and then act like the village fool the next. They can cuddle up for a nap with the family cat, and then go out and harass the rest of the neighborhood feline population. An Airedale can be exquisitely groomed and impressively handsome one day, and look like the Creature from the Black Lagoon the next. They display a wonderfully odd sense of playfulness at home, and then may turn dour when we want to show them off.

Airedales are well worth the work involved in raising, training, and maintaining them. They often go through a rocky puppyhood and adolescence, but they mellow into such fine companions that the troublesome times are forgotten by the time they mature. Slavish and robotic responses to commands are not in their nature, but once taught their lessons, they remember them well. (Admittedly, they may develop a temporary case of deafness to commands or requests on occasion, but they are undeniably one of the world's brightest breeds.) An Airedale's owner may never need to rely on the dog's instinctive hunting abilities, superior tracking talents, or remarkably protective nature, but these traits make the Airedale's personality what it is.

Airedales refuse to be ignored. Walk one into a group of people and children will appear from nowhere to pet this creature that looks so much like a big stuffed toy. Older folks will reminisce about Airedales they have known and will tell you that they were either the meanest dogs that ever lived, or the most wonderful. Come home from work bone-weary and depressed, and then attempt to take no notice of the Airedale joyfully watching your arrival through the window.

Why choose an Airedale Terrier when there are so many other breeds that are easier to raise, train, and live with? Why choose a breed that has such a pressing need for early socialization and training when there are so many placid breeds that rarely cause trouble? Why do some of us who work our dogs in the fields of Obedience, hunting, or Search and Rescue choose Airedales rather than breeds that specialize in these disciplines? The answer may be that Airedales attract a breed of person that is very similar to itself in temperament. We know that these characters are well worth the extra work it takes to develop our dogs into companions that mesh so well with our own personalities and lifestyles. We are aware of, and are willing to take on, all the responsibilities involved in owning just the right dog for us.

Useful Addresses and Literature

Health (Including First Aid), Breeding

Bordwell, Sally. *The American Animal Hospital Association Encyclopedia of Dog Health and Care*. New York: Hearst, 1994.

Faculty and Staff, School of Veterinary Medicine, University of California, Davis. *U.C. Davis Book of Dogs: A Complete Medical Reference Guide for Dogs and Puppies*. New York: Harper Collins, 1995.

Frye, Fredric. *First Aid for Your Dog*. Hauppauge, New York: Barron's Educational Series, Inc., 1987.

Kay, William J., DVM. *The Complete Book of Dog Health*. New York: Macmillan, 1995.

Holst, Phillis, DVM. *Canine Reproduction: A Breeder's Guide*. Loveland, CO: Alpine, 1985.

Homemade Diets for Dogs

Palika, Liz. *The Consumer's Guide to Dog Food*. New York: Howell Book House, 1996.

Pitcairn, Richard H., DVM, PhD and Pitcairn, Susan Hubble. *Dr. Pitcairn's Complete Guide to Natural Health for Dogs and Cats*. Emmaus, PA: Rodale Press, 1995.

General Books on Airedale Terriers

Cummins, Bryan. *The Working Airedale*. Centerville, AL: OTR, 1994.

Dutcher, June and Framke, Janet Johnson. *The New Airedale Terrier*. New York: Howell Book House, 1990.

Strebeigh, Barbara and McCready, Pauline J. *Your Airedale*. Fairfax, VA: Denlinger's, 1977.

Swash, Mary and Millar, Donald. *Airedale Terriers: An Owner's Companion*. Crowood (Great Britain), 1991.

Videotapes

American Kennel Club. *Airedale, AKC Breed Video*.

Dunbar Video Series. *Sirius Puppy Training*.

The Monks of New Skete. *Raising Your Dog With the Monks of New Skete*.

Clubs

The Airedale Terrier Club of America
Secretary: Ms. April Stevens
4078 Hickory Hill Road
Murrysville, PA 15666
(412) 327-4936

The Airedale Terrier Club of America
Hunting/Working Committee
Chairman: Steve Gilbert
100 Hawthorne Drive
Lima, OH 45805
(419) 991-7430
Web Site: http://www.dvcnet.com/atca/hwc

Airedale Terrier Club of Canada
Valerie Adkinson, Secretary
4044 Aberdeen Road
Beamsville, Ontario
Canada L0R 1B6
(905) 563-0539

Groomed for the show ring, or left "natural," the Airedale has a rough and ready look.

The American Kennel Club
51 Madison Avenue
New York, NY 10010
(212) 696-8200

The American Kennel Club
(Registration Information)
5580 Centerview Drive
Raleigh, NC 27606
(919) 233-9767

The United Kennel Club
100 East Kilgore Road
Kalamazoo, MI 49001-5598
(616) 343-9020

The Canadian Kennel Club
100-89 Skyway Avenue
Etobicoke, Ontario
Canada M9W 6R4
(416) 675-5511

The Orthopedic Foundation for
  Animals (OFA)
2300 Nifong Blvd.
Columbia, MO 65201
(573) 442-0418

Penn-Hip
Synbiotics Corporation
271 Great Valley Parkway
Malvern, PA 19355
(800) 248-8099

Canine Eye Registry
  Foundation (CERF)
South Campus Court, Building C
West Lafayette, IN 47907
(765) 494-8179

Arthur Wardle (English, 1864–1949) renowned for his portraiture of the Airedale, captured Ch. Dumbarton Lass in oil on canvas (top). His Airedale Head Studies (bottom) capture the independent, yet humorous, expression typical of the breed.

Index

The Airedale, largest of the terriers, is a rugged, energetic, loyal dog with a reputation for great courage. Bright, independent, and clever, this dog needs an owner who enjoys work and play as much as his pet. The Airedale approaches life with great enthusiasm, whether hunting and retrieving, gaiting in the show ring, or playing ball with its family. If you are an active individual with a zest for life and time to properly train, groom, and love your pet, the Airedale may be the dog for you.